EXCAVATIONS

IN THE

TOMBS OF THE KINGS.

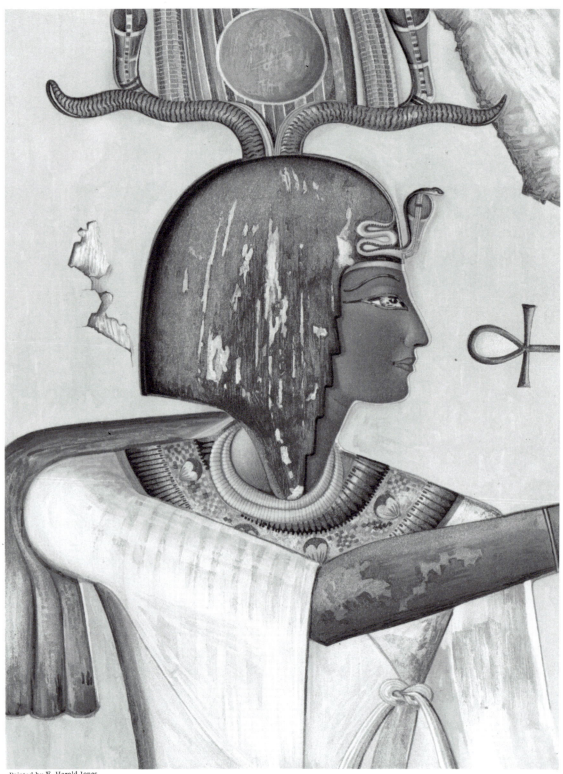

Painted by E. Harold Jones

SIPTAH

THEODORE M. DAVIS'

EXCAVATIONS: BIBÂN EL MOLÛK.

THE TOMB OF SIPHTAH;
THE MONKEY TOMB AND THE GOLD TOMB.

THE DISCOVERY OF THE TOMBS,

BY

THEODORE M. DAVIS.

KING SIPHTAH AND QUEEN TAUOSRÎT,

BY

GASTON MASPERO.

THE EXCAVATIONS OF 1905–1907,

BY

EDWARD AYRTON.

CATALOGUE OF THE OBJECTS DISCOVERED,

BY

GEORGE DARESSY.

ILLUSTRATIONS

BY

E. HAROLD JONES.

Duckworth

The Tomb of Siphtah first published in 1908
The Tomb of Queen Tîyi first published in 1910
by Archibald Constable & Co. Ltd.
Reprinted in one volume in 2001 by
Gerald Duckworth & Co. Ltd.
61 Frith Street, London W1D 3JL
Tel: 020 7434 4242
Fax: 020 7434 4420
Email: enquiries@duckworth-publishers.co.uk
www.ducknet.co.uk

A catalogue record for this book is available
from the British Library

ISBN 0 7156 3073 3

Printed in Great Britain by Bath Press, Bath

FOREWORD

'... there before us lay the [gilded and inlaid coffin] of Tîyi [Tiye]. It was the most thrilling sight I ever beheld. Arrayed as she might have been when Amenhotep the Magnificent led her to the marriage feast, there she lay, with arms folded, and that immovable expression on her face which the contemplation of the vanity of all things might have produced. Dazzled by the splendour of this sight I did not at first notice that the side of the coffin had fallen out, and that alongside this gorgeous effigy lay the real body of the queen. Her dried-up face, sunken cheeks, and thin, leathery looking lips, exposing a few teeth, were in ghastly contrast to the golden diadem which encircled her head and the gold necklace that partially hid her shrunken throat ...

*

I wrote the above account while the excitement of this dramatic find was filling our minds, and while our enthusiasm was untroubled by any doubts as to its authenticity ... But a sad disillusionment was in store. Since I left Egypt this interesting mummy has been examined by expert surgeons in addition to the Egyptologists, and the skeleton has proved to be that of a young man ...'

(Walter Tyndale, *Below the Cataracts* London, 1907, pp. 194-5)

The excavations carried out between 1902 and 1914 by American amateur archaeologist Theodore M. Davis are among the most significant in the history of exploration in the Valley of the Kings; they resulted in the discovery and/or documentation of an astonishing thirty and more tombs and pits, of which two-thirds were cleared during the 'golden age' of Davis's explorations — the years 1905-1908. The most significant of these finds would be published in two splendid reports: *The Tomb of Siphtah; the Monkey Tomb and the Gold Tomb* (London, 1908) and *The Tomb of Queen Tîyi* (London, 1910).

The first of these volumes represents a treasure-trove of material for archaeologists today, documenting not only Davis's initial probings into the tomb of the 19th Dynasty king 'Siphtah' [Siptah] — a project not completed until 1913 — but most of his 'lesser' finds also. Among these smaller tombs, nos 50, 51 and 52 contained an extraordinary collection of royal pets — a dog, monkeys, baboons, and several ducks, all carefully embalmed in the Egyptian manner and remarkably lifelike. Most significant of all, however, was the 'Gold Tomb' (no. 56) — so labelled when clearance of this mud-filled chamber yielded the greatest cache of 19th Dynasty precious jewellery ever found.

The Tomb of Queen Tîyi documents the discovery, on 6 January 1907, of a mysterious, single-chambered corridor tomb. Initially identified as the burial of Amenophis III's queen, Tiye [Tîyi] — on the basis of a spectacular gilded-wood shrine found within — the body itself was subsequently recognised as that of a *man*, buried in a woman's coffin which had been adapted for the use of an Amarna-period pharaoh. Was this the mummy of Akhenaten himself, as some at the time believed, and indeed still believe? Or the body of Akhenaten's mysterious coregent, Smenkhkare? Almost a century on, 'Tomb 55' continues to baffle archaeologist and Egyptologist alike.

For the background to the Tomb 55 controversy, readers are referred to C.N. Reeves, *Valley of the Kings: The decline of a royal necropolis* (London, 1990), pp. 42-49 and 55-60 and to my 'Archaeological Analysis of KV55, 1907-1990', which introduced an earlier, revised reprint of Davis's report — *The Tomb of Queen Tîyi* (San Francisco, 1990), pp. iv-xiv.

London, January 2001   Nicholas Reeves

CONTENTS.

PREFACE.

I DESIRE to renew my expression of gratitude to Monsieur Maspero for his kindness in writing the Life of Siphtah.

I also congratulate E. Harold Jones upon his artistic success as evidenced by the reproductions of his drawings.

THEODORE M. DAVIS.

NEWPORT,
    RHODE ISLAND,
        U.S.A.

LIST OF ILLUSTRATIONS.

LIST OF PLANS.

KING SIPHTAH AND QUEEN TAUOSRÎT.

to M. Maspero my proposed manner of exploration, he replied, "it will require money, perseverance, and patience, I am not sure about the latter." I accept M. Maspero's requirements, but I would add Hope to his catalogue.

In November, 1905, I fortunately was able to secure the services of Edward R. Ayrton as my assistant; his knowledge of cataloguing, keen observation, and willingness to live in the "valley," that he might be present when the men were working, thereby securing thorough and honest work, rendered his services most valuable.

On the 18th December, 1905, we got our first sight of a tomb, which, on 21st inst., proved to be Siphtah's (Meneptah II), a king of the XIXth Dynasty.

The success of my exploration theory is demonstrated by the following incident: the site of the tomb was most unpromising; nevertheless it required its clearing; the Government Rais, who many years ago explored for the Cairo Museum, chanced to be present during the first day of our work, and volunteered the information that "he had thoroughly explored, some years ago, the same hill, and he knew there was no tomb in it." A day or two thereafter we found the tomb; then the Rais told us that he knew where there were several other tombs on the hill, and that he would show them to us! In behalf of the Rais I ought to say that he, doubtless, had explored the site, but, after his old manner of work, failed to discover the tomb; his statement of the existence of various tombs was an Arabic fantasy intended to please us.

The finding of this tomb contributes to the knowledge of the history of the last years of the XIXth Dynasty, inasmuch as it proves that Siphtah had a tomb of his own, and was not, as formerly supposed, buried in the tomb of his wife Tauosrît. If Siphtah did no great deeds during his reign, he would seem to have possessed extremely good taste in the decoration of his tomb, and causing to be made for himself a beautiful alabaster sarcophagus; a fragment of which only remains, as will be seen by the illustrations herewith published.

UNNAMED TOMB.

My excuse for the publication of the finding in January, 1908, of an unnamed tomb, in connection with my work in 1905 and 1906, is that the contents of the tomb reveal interesting knowledge respecting the relations of Setui II, Queen Tauosrît, and Siphtah, and permits me, at an early date, to publish reproductions of the unique deposits of gold and silver ornaments.

In the process of exhausting the possibilities of the " foot-hill," which is opposite our last explored site, we commenced our quest on January 3rd, 1908. Clearing the " foot-hill" of all the stones and débris, and, finding nothing, we reached the wide path which is founded on the original water course of the valley, and started to follow down the vertical rock. After a few days' work, with a large number of men and boys, to our surprise we found that the rock continued to descend vertically, with no signs of " flatting." I frankly admit it seemed a waste of time and expense, but I determined to follow the rock as long as it remained perpendicular, therefore we continued our descent for several days. I was conscious, however, that we had reached a point below the water course of the ancient valley, and that, if any tomb existed, its contents must have been destroyed. The result, however, was that, after descending twenty-eight feet from the surface of our starting point, we were rewarded by the discovery of a tomb cut in the still persisting perpendicular rock. It proved to be without decorations or inscriptions, and consisted of one room, twenty-five feet wide and ten feet high. It was nearly filled with very hard mud, which had evidently been washed in by the ancient waters. Doubtless the unknown man who excavated it paid no attention to the fact that it would be flooded by the subsequent rain storms, until he realised that his mummy could not be preserved for resurrection, therefore he seems to have abandoned the tomb.[1]

There was nothing in sight, or promise, of any objects having been deposited in the tomb, but, as a matter of course, we undertook to clear it, using carving knives to break up the mud, as we feared that the use of heavy implements would destroy any possible deposits. As none of our workmen were allowed in the tomb, Mr. Ayrton did this most disagreeable work with his own hands—a task requiring skill, endurance, and patience.

On the second day of Mr. Ayrton's labour, I made my usual daily visit to the Valley of the Kings, and on my arrival Mr. Ayrton told me that, shortly before finishing the morning's work, he had discovered a very small morsel of gold buried in the mud. We delayed our entrance for an hour or two, but, had we for a moment supposed that the tomb contained the wonderful deposit which we now know, I am quite sure there would have been no delay.

---

[1] I have found two or three instances of commencements of tombs in the water courses, which, after some progress had been made, had been abandoned, evidently fearing the water.

When we entered the tomb we were able, with the aid of two candles, to see the bit of gold, but it was so embedded in the mud we dared not use the carving knives, fearing they would injure the object. We, therefore, procured water and flooded the spot where the hard mud held the gold, and presently disclosed the two beautiful gold ear-rings, or wig-rings, illustrated in the catalogue. During the afternoon we flooded a space about four feet square, and, before dark, found nearly all the objects hereafter described.

Among the objects was a pair of silver gloves, evidently intended for a woman with small hands. I dissolved the mud with which they were filled by soaking the gloves in water, and when I poured out the contents there came eight unique gold finger rings, with cartouches of Setuî II, Queen Tauosrît, and Rameses II.

The total result of our work was : the finding of a collection of unique gold and silver jewellery, three thousand years old, practically in as good condition as it was the day it was made : the final settlement of the period of Setuî II and his relation to Tauosrît.

THE ANIMAL TOMBS.

In the month of January, 1906, we resumed our policy of clearing. We began our work on a foot-hill near the tomb of " Siphtah," and, on the 31st inst., discovered two " Pit-tombs." The first one had a perpendicular shaft, 12 feet deep, cut in the rock and filled with stones and débris ; it opened into a room 8 feet square and 5 feet high. I went down the shaft and entered the chamber, which proved to be extremely hot and too low for comfort. I was startled by seeing very near me a yellow dog of ordinary size standing on his feet, his short tail curled over his back, and his eyes open. Within a few inches of his nose sat a monkey in quite perfect condition ; for an instant I thought they were alive, but I soon saw that they had been mummified, and that they had been unwrapped in ancient times by robbers. Evidently they had taken a fragment of the wooden monkey-box, on which they seated the monkey to keep him upright, and then they stood the dog on his feet so near the monkey, that his nose nearly touched him.

The attitude of the animals suggested that the monkey was saying, " It's all over with me," and the dog, with his bright eyes and manner, seemed to reply, " Have courage, it will end all right." I am quite sure the robbers arranged the group for their amusement. However this may be, it can fairly be said to be a joke 3000 years old.

Subsequently we entered the second "Pit-tomb," which was very near the first, and practically of the same order. It also contained mummified monkeys, birds, ducks, etc., full details of which will be found in Mr. Ayrton's report.

The tomb of Amenhotep II being so near the "Pit-tombs," it is quite possible that the mummified animals were originally the King's pets.

In the course of our exploration of the foot-hills, which included the discovery of the animals referred to above, we found that, many years ago, some government explorer had adopted the method of sinking a narrow pit through the overlying débris to the rock, and, finding nothing, moved on about 12 feet, and there pitted as formerly; this manner of exploring he continued until he had finished the hill.

We discovered that his narrow pits, in several instances, came within a few inches of the tombs we found, thereby showing the advantage of exhausting the possibilities of a location.

THE TOMB OF MENTU HER KHEPSHEF.

This tomb was opened and robbed in ancient times. For many years it was filled with débris; thinking its clearing might be instructive, I decided to have it done. Mr. Ayrton's report will give full details.

THE EXCAVATIONS DURING THE WINTERS OF 1905–1906.

T. M. DAVIS AND E. R. AYRTON.

WE recommenced our work this year towards the end of October, 1905, at the same spot where it had been left off last season.

The promontory of rock in which Tomb No. 12 is situated had been partially dug over on its southern face. We spent some three days in excavating the upper layers of rubbish here. No results, however, were forthcoming, and we removed our work to the extreme east of the valley, slightly to the south of the tomb of Thothmes IV, with the intention of, later, completing the first site. Here we dug up the slope to the face of the cliffs, finding nothing except the unfinished entrance to a tomb which had barely been begun.

The spot next chosen was in front of Uaa and Thuaa's tomb, where we ran long trenches, working down to the bed-rock, from east to west across the front of Tomb No. 3. We then turned to north and south along the rock face, but with no results. To the north the sloping rock suddenly dips down at a perpendicular angle to form the main water-course, and, since it was obvious that no tomb could ever have been made there, we shifted our work to the opposite side of the tourist path, and began to dig in front of the tomb of Rameses IV. The ground in front of this tomb had at first the appearance of being untouched desert surface, covered with black flints, but, on digging one or two trial pits, we found that in reality the rock came to an abrupt end at a distance of about twenty feet from the mouth of the tomb, and went down perpendicularly to a depth of some twelve feet. This had been filled up level to the upper surface with the masons' rubbish from a tomb. The broken vessels and dishes of the workmen had also been thrown in, and the whole covered with flints from the real desert surface to give it a natural appearance, and to hide one of the most important witnesses to the presence of a tomb.

We removed the greater part of this débris to see if it concealed an older tomb, but were unsuccessful. A series of ostraka, however, rewarded our efforts to some extent. These are all drawn or painted on pieces of white limestone, which offer a good surface for such work. Of these the best is probably that of a king's head, wearing the ringed war helmet. The face is coloured a light pink, the helmet being black. A sketch plan of the door of a tomb (probably No. 2) with, on the reverse, a design showing a lion holding a captive's head in its mouth, is well done. Some lines of a formula in hieratic with the name of Amenhotep I, an ostrakon mentioning Neb-hapet Ra Mentuhotep, the head of a Libyan, and a horse and chariot, were also found here, the two latter being drawn in red ink.

Almost all the masons' pottery had been broken up into small fragments before it was buried, only a few shallow dishes remaining entire. These were encrusted with plaster, and, in some cases, with colours which had been used in the decoration of the tomb. Most of the pots had marks scratched on them, which are interesting, since their date is quite certain. As several fragments bear the name of Rameses II, and no other name appears on them, it is probable that this rubbish is all from his tomb.

We next worked up towards the mouth of the tomb of Rameses IV on the north, and dug through the débris of rough Coptic and Roman huts, which had been occupied by the plunderers of this tomb. There we found some dozens of fragments and about twenty specimens of alabaster ushabtis of Rameses IV, very roughly cut, some being blocked out without any attempt at detail; the features, a line of hieroglyphs, and the cartouches of the king being carelessly painted in. Fragments of Coptic ostraka and one unopened papyrus letter were also unearthed. The Coptic house was roughly built of fragments of limestone; the walls cannot have been of any great height, and the rooms were very small. The Roman house beneath was built of sun-dried bricks, with a floor of baked bricks and stone. In front of this was a small oven and two small circular granaries; at one end of the house three amphorae used for storing honey were found; the ends had been knocked off, and they were filled with the comb.

Removing these huts, we dug some three feet through the limestone chippings to the rock level.

Our work was next shifted to the northern face of the promontory of rock which runs out from the perpendicular cliffs slightly south of the tomb of

Amenhotep II.   Here the rock goes down almost perpendicularly to a depth of some thirteen feet below the present surface.   We dug along the whole length of this, our only finds being one or two ostraka of the XXth Dynasty.

The results here were disappointing.   We were, however, more fortunate towards the eastern point of the promontory, where at a depth of twelve feet from the surface we found a beautiful blue-glazed cup, bearing the cartouche of Tutankhamen of the XVIIIth Dynasty.   On the bottom of the cup were four nobs of pottery, probably to stand the cup free from the flat bottom. The cup, when found, was protected by a large overhanging stone.   Evidently the water had rushed in enough débris to hold it in place, thereby preserving it.   Why, or from what cause it made such a perilous journey, is, of course, unknown.

At a higher level, somewhat to the east of this, and only three feet from the surface, we found a group of fourteen ushabtis of Rameses IV, exactly similar to those found outside his tomb ; these were probably hidden here by modern thieves or plunderers.

Our next step resulted in the discovery of the tomb of Siphtah, which is described in the following chapter.

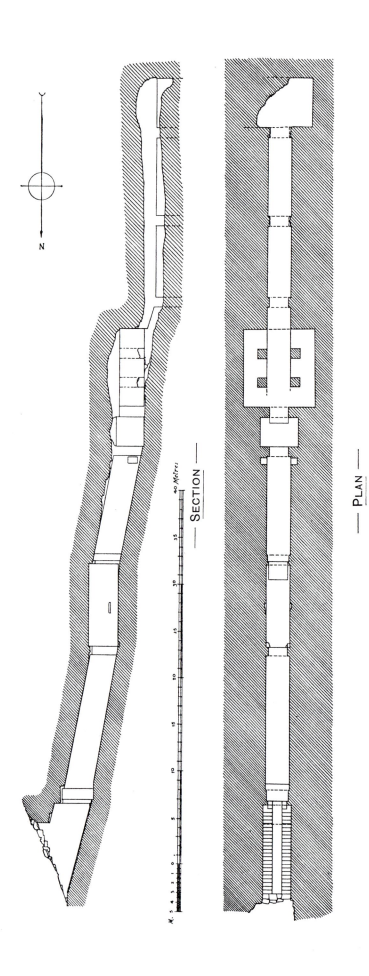

N

SECTION

40 Metres

PLAN

— TOMB OF SIPHTAH —

THE TOMB OF SIPHTAH MERENPTAH.

THE southern extremity of the Royal Valley tapers off into a narrow water channel. Just to the north of this, and to the west, the cliffs form a large bay partially separated from the main valley by a long tongue of rock, which starts from the perpendicular cliffs on the south. In this bay are situated a family group of tombs of the XIXth Dynasty—Setuî II, Tauosrît, Bai, and the newly-discovered tomb of Siphtah. The three former are hollowed out of the actual face of the cliff; that of Siphtah runs into the tongue of rock from north to south.

The stonemasons' rubbish from the tombs of Setuî II and Tauosrît, with probably a certain amount of débris from that of Siphtah, had been thrown on to and against this promontory. This rubbish, after many centuries, had silted down and thus hidden the entrance to the tomb with a level layer varying in depth from six to twelve feet; there were, therefore, no indications of any sort to lead us to suppose that a tomb had ever been made in this place.

As our plan, however, was to leave no spot, even the most unpromising, without a trial, we ran trenches at every few feet towards the rock, and finding that this sloped up at a gradual angle, we lengthened our trenches, and were soon rewarded by striking the top of a flight of steps leading into a tomb.

At once every available workman was set to work, and, after a day's hard labour we were able to catch a glimpse of the door lintel, and to read the cartouches of Siphtah, a king who has always been thought to share with Tauosrît the tomb which lies opposite (No. 14).

The plan of the tomb (Page 10 : Tomb of Siphtah) is in the general style of the late XIXth and early XXth dynasties. Two shallow flights of steps, with a sloping plane between, lead down to the entrance, the flanking rock being covered by white stucco, but unornamented. These steps are made of carefully cut blocks, inserted after the slope had been cut, and are not part

of the solid rock.   The slope leads down to the entrance proper of the tomb—
a large doorway coated with stucco and ornamented in the usual way with
the king's titles down each jamb, and a mythological scene on the lintel.

As will be seen from the photograph (Plate : Entrance to the Tomb of
King Siphtah) the lintel was originally supported by a beam of wood ; the
holes in the floor and roof—sockets for a large wooden bivalve door—are
also there.   This is the case with each of the further doors.

After this first doorway, we pass through three long corridors, the first and
last sloping at an angle, and the central one being horizontal.   Of these the
first two are coated with stucco and are covered with scenes and hieroglyphs
in colour, the roofs being also decorated ; but beyond this no trace of stucco
remains.   The third corridor has at its further end two small recesses, one in
each wall.

Passing through a square chamber, with a horizontal floor, one enters a
large hall, the roof of which was originally supported by four columns.   Only
one of these remains at present, and this we were obliged to prop up as a
slight shock would have been quite sufficient to make it fall.   The floor at
the sides and the roof are horizontal, but in the centre a cutting leads down
into a corridor, the roof of which is below the horizontal floor-level of the
hall.   Beyond this are two corridors leading into a square room.

We penetrated below it far enough to ascertain that there was another
chamber in which the invading water had deposited a solid mass of débris
many feet high ; in most places the roof had fallen in, exposing a cavity quite
two metres high, thereby rendering the chamber most unsafe to work in.

We knew that the mummy of the king had been found by Loret some
years ago in the tomb of Amenhotep II.   In addition to this, it was evident
that the tomb had been completely plundered in ancient times, and if any
objects had been left in the room they must have been crushed beyond
recognition by the weight of the mass of rock which had filled the chamber.

The discovery of a fragment of an alabaster sarcophagus, which we found
the first day we entered the corridor, convinced us that destruction would
pervade the tomb.   We therefore decided to abandon the excavations.

The flight of steps at the entrance, as we have already mentioned, was
filled with rubbish, but this rubbish belonged to two different periods.   The
lower mound which reached almost to the door lintel was the earlier, and
had originally filled the entrance more or less completely, but an entrance
had been dug down through this, by later plunderers or priests, which in turn
had silted up.   In this lower rubbish were pots and pans in a more or less

broken condition, of the type which was used by workmen on a tomb. These could not have belonged to Siphtah, since, as we shall see, this rubbish was very much later than the burial of the king, and must have been thrown in from some other tomb. The pottery appears to belong to the XIXth or XXth Dynasties. One of the fragments bears the name of Setuî-Merenptah; a pot is exactly similar to one found by Petrie in Tauosrît's funerary temple, and two or three of the larger ones are similar to those found in the masons' rubbish of Ramses II.

An interesting point, worthy of consideration, is that the cartouches throughout Siphtah's tomb have been cut out and again restored, and, since this rubbish completely covered several of the restored cartouches both at the entrance and in the corridor, this rubbish must have been deposited here after the restoration had taken place.

That this rubbish completely filled the entrance is clear, since we found a rough chip-wall built on top of the mound to hold back the rubbish dug out by the next people to enter the place. A deeper passage had then been scooped in the rubbish in the first corridor, the débris being thrown against the west wall, and on top of this rubbish were lying fragments of an alabaster sarcophagus and also a ushabti of Siphtah. In the second corridor were found pieces of ushabtis *under* the stucco which had dropped from the walls.

In the rubbish we found fragments of blue glazed ushabtis, one of which bears the cartouche of Men-mat-Ra, but by the glaze it is probably of later date than Setuî I, and also pieces of well-cut ushabtis in alabaster. In this upper rubbish, and with the pottery below, we found numerous fragments of ostraka, one or two of which bear the name of Setuî II, whilst three bear dates, and the rest refer to lists of workmen, receipts, or bear single names.

On the floor of the second corridor below the water-laid rubbish was found a piece of wood with the inscription The Royal Mother Thïy, the hieroglyphs being incised and inlaid with blue paint. Besides the ushabtis of Siphtah, we found the upper part of an ushabti of a woman in alabaster, and of better workmanship than those of Siphtah.

DESCRIPTION OF DECORATION.

The entrance slope with its flight of steps is only coated with a layer of white stucco, which has been left plain.

On the lintel of the entrance is depicted the worship of the Sun, in his form of Khnum-kheper-Ra, by Isis and Nephthys; behind Isis is an invocation to Ra-Horakhti for the Royal Osirian, and behind Nephthys is a similar prayer to Osiris for the king. The whole of this scene rests on a conventional bed of sand. On the outer side of each jamb are the full titles of the king, with his two Horus names, Ka-nekht-meri-Hapi and Ka-nekht-ur-pehti.

Immediately inside the entrance, on both sides of the door, is a scene of the goddess Maat with wings outstretched, above whom are three lines of hieroglyphs and the cartouches of the king; she is seated on a large neb basket, which is supported on the flowers of a papyrus plant on one side of the door, and a lotus on the other. These scenes occupy the whole height of the wall, and are on a slightly higher level than the true wall of the corridor. Beyond this, on the left, is a very finely worked scene of the king receiving Life, Power, and Strength from Ra Harmachis (Plate : "Entrance to the Tomb of King Siphtah"). Between them are the cartouches of the king and the titles of the god.

These cartouches have been erased and replaced with great care, as have also the smaller cartouches on the belt of the king. The head of the king is especially good, being quite perfect, and is the only real portrait we possess of this monarch.

After this scene, the first two corridors of the tomb are decorated with texts which are collectively called by the name of "The Litany of the Sun." The Litany begins with three vertical lines of hieroglyphs, giving the title of the first chapter or book. Then follows a scene (Plate : "The Flight of the Evil Demons before the Sun"), which shows the Sun as Khnum-Kheper-Ra sinking between the two horizons, whilst the evil demons of Amentet fly before him towards the head of a gazelle with a flame between its horns, emblematical of the Underworld.

On the same wall we find seventy-five vertical lines of hieroglyphs, each of which forms a separate adoration of some form of the god Ra. The remainder of the wall, and the left-hand jamb of the second doorway, are covered with eighty-one vertical lines of hieroglyphs, forming a short hymn, which states that the deceased knows all that is contained in the seventy-five preceding adorations.

The first part of both walls of the second corridor is divided into two registers. In the upper are shown seventy-five personages, each with his name, which correspond to the adorations in the first corridor.

The lower register of the two walls of the second corridor is partly filled with a short text in vertical lines, forming Chapter 2 of the Litany. This is addressed to the gods who inhabit the various spheres of the Underworld, and is somewhat similar to Chapter 127 of the Book of the Dead.

We now return to the first corridor, the right-hand wall of which begins with Chapter III, and which is composed of fifteen vertical lines, and is merely a short invocation.

Next come vertical lines forming the fourth chapter of our Litany, which ends on the ceiling of the second corridor.

Filling the southern end of the second corridor, on both walls, is the vignette of Chapter 151 of the Book of the Dead; Anubis (Plate: Anubis) bends over the mummy of the deceased on his couch, at the head and foot of which kneel Isis (Plate: Isis) and Nephthys, leaning forward and resting their hands on the emblem of eternity. In the four corners of the scene stand the genii of Amentet (Hapi, Qebhsennuf, Amset, and Duamutef), whilst Anubis Amiut on his shrine rests above and below the funeral couch. In the third hall the water has almost completely destroyed the stucco, and it is only from a few loose scraps near the door that we are able to know that it was once decorated with scenes from the book of Amduat, of which the fourth chapter began on the right-hand wall.

The ceiling of the first corridor (Plate: Ceiling in Main Corridor) is of the same design as those in the tombs of Setuî I and Setuî II. Vultures with natural heads, or the head of a snake, with outspread wings and grasping a fan in their claws, stretch across the breadth of the ceiling, and alternate with the royal cartouches, whilst down each side runs a long line of hieroglyphs painted in colours on a yellow background. This ceiling is damaged near the doorway, but enough remains within to give a very good idea of the design and colouring. The ceiling of the second hall is quite perfect, and shows a background of black with yellow stars, and, in the centre, a long oblong of yellow on which are thirty-four lines of grey hieroglyphs from the final chapter of the Litany of the Sun, and a vignette showing the soul of the Sun-god, represented by a ram-headed bird on a disc between two blood-red hawks, with respectively the emblems of Isis and Nephthys on their heads, standing on two shrines or pylons. The ceiling of the third corridor was probably similar to that of the second, but it has been completely destroyed.

No traces of further decoration remain in the tomb, though one or two hieroglyphs in the further rooms show that it was originally finished.

PRIVATE TOMBS.

THE approach to the tomb of Amenhotep II (No. 35) is through a small wadi formed by two rock promontories, which jut out to the east from the perpendicular cliffs on the west of the Royal Valley, and near to its southern end. The promontory to the north of this wadi is occupied by Tombs Nos. 12 and 9. The southern promontory had not yet been touched. This presented to the eye a level surface of loose rubbish, unbroken by depressions. According to our system of exhaustion we sank pits at the eastern end to find the rock level, and then commenced a complete clearance of the slope working towards the west. We were rewarded by the discovery of five tombs, which, although plundered and of no great size, yielded interesting results.

The first of these sepulchres (No. 49) was situated on the northern side of the promontory, and ran into the rock towards the south. The entrance was filled with loose limestone chips, and amongst these we found a large fragment of limestone showing an official worshipping, and also, on another chip of limestone, a design in red and black of a man offering to Queen Aahmes-Nefertari.

In date it is probably of the XVIIIth Dynasty. A flight of steps leads down to the doorway which opens into a long sloping corridor, at the other end of which is another doorway which shows signs of having been sealed up with stones and cement. This opens into a large rectangular room in the floor of which a staircase was begun, leading down, but never finished. The staircase had been filled with rubbish to the level of the floor of the room, and the burial probably took place here. The only objects in the room were a few scraps of mummy-cloth and fragments of the large whitened jars which occur in burials of the XVIIIth Dynasty. Plunderers had dug a small pit in the second stairway to search for a further door, and in this rubbish we found a very fine ostrakon of "Hay, the chief of the workmen in the Place of Truth" (a name of this portion of the Theban necropolis). On the obverse he makes offerings at an altar to a huge snake, Mer-segr ("Lover of Silence"), the Goddess of the Tombs. On the reverse is a well-written hieratic inscription giving a list of workmen. Several very rough limestone slabs with squares scratched on them for a game were also found in the chamber. Over the first entrance to the tomb is a list of workmen written in red hieratic characters.

To the west of this tomb, and on a slightly higher level of the same tongue of rock, we discovered a group of three pit-tombs, forming a rough triangle. All were covered with rubbish to a depth of six feet, and the shafts were also filled with débris. The plan was in each case the same—a short square shaft, of no great depth, from the southern side of which a chamber was cut into the rock; this varied in size in the three tombs, but was in no case very large.

In the first tomb opened (No. 50), the chamber was about 19 feet long by 6–8 feet broad. The shaft, 12 feet deep by about 4 feet square, was full of rubbish, some of which had penetrated into the room. It had been almost completely plundered, only a few fragments of wood remaining from the coffin. Propped up against the eastern wall was a large dog, quite perfect although stripped of its wrappings, and a monkey still partially wrapped. This type of dog is described by Daressy and Gaillard in the Cairo Catalogue (*Faune de l'Anc. Egypte* (1), 29,501). Unfortunately we could find no trace of the name of the owner of the tomb.

The second tomb (No. 51) of the group, situated slightly to the north of this, consisted of a short shaft with a very small chamber opening to the south. This had been plundered, and some of the rubbish from the shaft had found its way into the chamber; the entrance had been closed up again with bits of stone, and part of the disused lid of a mummy coffin.

The chamber was completely filled with animals, all of which had been originally mummified and done up in cloth wrappings. On the right on entering were two monkeys, placed with their backs to the wall in a squatting position, one completely wrapped up, the other with apparently burnt wrappings partly torn from the face and head. Against the south wall was a large monkey, with the wrappings torn from its head, a tarred box-coffin for some animal, and a heap of loose bandages in which was the unwrapped body of an ibis. Against the east wall in the corner was a perfect specimen of a large cynocephalous ape, wearing a necklace of small blue disc beads.

5.

Three mummified ducks were also found in the chamber, as well as some bundles of intestines made up in the form of little human figures ; one of these had near it a mask of beautifully coloured stucco, representing a human head, which had probably originally fitted it. This was certainly of the XVIIIth Dynasty.

In most cases the wrappings had been torn off, and in other cases the cloth had been pulled away from the neck to remove any jewellery, etc., which had been worn by the animal.

The third tomb (No. 52) consisted of a shaft 9 feet 6 inches deep, and a chamber 8 × 5 feet and 4 feet 8 inches high, was absolutely empty except for two boxes, one of which was almost double the size of the other. These were covered with bitumen and were without decoration or ornament either inside or out. The larger contained numerous loose wrappings and the unwrapped body of a small monkey ; the smaller box was divided into four partitions, resembling in this respect a box for canopic jars.

To the west of the two last-mentioned tombs, and on the same slope, was another tomb (No. 48) of the same type. The shaft was about 20 feet deep by 6 feet broad, with a comparatively large chamber, 16–17 feet by 10–11 feet by 6 feet high, to the south-west. The tomb had been anciently plundered, but a rough wall had been re-constructed to close the chamber door. The floor was covered with some six inches of rubbish, and on this lay the débris from the burial. The mummy, that of a man, tall and well-built, had been unwrapped and thrown on one side. Fragments of the coffin, which was of wood coated with pitch and then painted with yellow hieroglyphs, lay scattered about the floor. We were so fortunate, on sifting the rubbish on the ground, as to discover some wooden ushabtis with the titles of Amonmapt, Vizier and Governor of the Town, painted in yellow on a surface of pitch. Three perfect and fragments of another mud tablet, which had originally been wrapped in tarred cloth, also bore the name and titles of the vizier. A clay seal from a roll of papyrus (?) bearing the inscription " Amen hears good praises," was also found. Fragments of a rough wooden chair and pieces of white pottery jars lay scattered about. On the whole, the furniture must have been very poor when compared with the rank of the man, and the walls of the tomb were quite bare, without even a layer of stucco to fill the irregularities of the rock.

On the other side of the path, and slightly to the north of Tomb 29, we discovered another burial-place (No. 53). This consisted of a square shallow shaft, leading down to a large room. The tomb had been plundered, and nothing was found in the chamber except an ostrakon of one "Hora, chief scribe in the Place of Truth." In the rubbish of the shaft were found several ostraka.

The remains of rough workmen's huts were near by, and had been built over the mouth of the tomb, which had, however, been since plundered; and built into the walls of one of these we discovered several ostraka and trial pieces, most of which had suffered considerably from exposure to the elements.

THE TOMB OF RAMESES MENTUHERKHEPSHEF.

(No. 19.)

E. R. AYRTON.

THE tomb of Prince Rameses Mentuherkhepshef is situated immediately under the cliffs which shut in the eastern side of the Royal Valley at Thebes, and occupies, at a lower level, the space between the sepulchres of Thothmes IV and Hatshepsut.

It runs into a tongue of land which juts out to a short distance and at a steep angle from the perpendicular cliffs. A dry water-channel runs down from the upper plateau, drops some distance perpendicularly, and then goes along the southern side of this promontory, turning round the point and continuing north-west directly in front of the entrance of the tomb.

The tomb has been known for some time to European savants, and various descriptions have been published. The earliest description which we have is that of Champollion (*Notices*, p. 464), who describes it as the tomb of Prince Rameses. From his notes, we see that the doorway was practically clear of rubbish, since he gives a sketch of the rough hieroglyphs on the outer side of the southern jamb; the first scenes on either side of the corridor were, however, more or less blocked; the second were partly clear, and the rest of the tomb was probably in much the same state as when examined by Lefèbre. After giving details of the various gods and the offerings before them, Champollion says that the "corridor led to a square "hall in which the mummy of the prince had once lain, some fragments "of which we found here." Numerous fragments of black stone, which probably belonged to the sarcophagus, were also found here.

The tomb was next visited by Lepsius (*L.D.*, III, 216, 217 A–D) and two complete scenes are published by him. He also gives two examples of the titles borne by the prince, and full-sized coloured portrait.

Later again the tomb was visited by Lefèbre (*Mission arch. francaise*, 1889, III, 164 and plates), who gives a more detailed account. He found the tomb filled with blocks of stone and the entrance obstructed by a huge

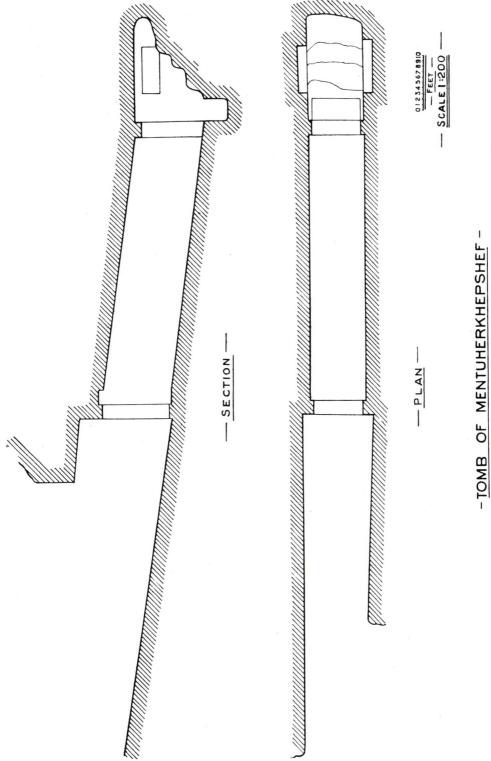

— SECTION —

— PLAN —

0 1 2 3 4 5 6 7 8 9 10
— FEET —
— SCALE 1:200 —

— TOMB OF MENTUHERKHEPSHEF —

Scene 7.

The prince worships a goddess with a cat's head, who wears the red disk surrounded by a serpent. She is called :

Behind the goddess is an invocation for the prince, who is called :

In the corridor over these scenes are numerous roughly-scratched graffiti.

Situated as the tomb is at the foot of a path which leads up to a narrow couloir (with numerous graffiti) to the top of a plateau, and over to Deir el Bahri, it would form a very convenient resting-place for guards or plunderers.

Not many portable antiquities were found in the tomb. Several ostraka were, however, unearthed in the entrance. The most important of these was a large block of flinty limestone, with a long religious inscription written in black ink, with the cartouches of Rameses Ra-hak-maat ; this was found between the stone wall and the entrance, some six feet from the ground, and there was consequently nothing to prove its connection with the filling of the tomb, as this part had probably been dug over several times. From the entrance of the tomb, at various levels in the débris, we found the small glazed objects of a foundation deposit, also an alabaster plaque with the cartouche ⬚, and a small blue glazed plaque in the shape of a cartouche with the name Ra-hak-maat ; several small beads were also found.

In the entrance filling was found a slip of limestone with the cartouches of Rameses Ra-kheper-maat. A few fragments of pottery vases were found in and near the burial pit, also the upper part of a broken mummy.

Several fragments of a long stela of a *sedem ash* in "The Place of Truth" (*i.e.*, Theban Necropolis) named Hay were found in various parts of the tomb ; they all join together and fit another piece found in the Coptic midden outside the tomb of Rameses IV (No. 2 in the valley). This is important, since it furnishes us with a possible solution of how a foundation deposit of Rameses IV came to be scattered about the tomb of Mentuherkhepshef. It should be noticed that, in the earlier part of the season, whilst digging outside the tomb of Rameses IV, we found his foundation deposit, which only consisted of wooden objects, which obviously formed part of an originally larger deposit. It seems probable that the tomb of the prince was used as a caravanserai by various tomb robbers, situated as it is at what must have been the quickest road to and from the valley, and it seems not unlikely that the robbers were engaged in plundering, amongst others, the tomb of Rameses IV. Hay's stela suffered in much the same way as the deposit, as we have already seen.

In 1885, Lefèbre published in the *Zeitschrift für Äg. Sprache* (vol. XXIII, p. 125) his theories for supposing that this Mentuherkhepshef was not the same prince as the Mentuherkhepshef shown amongst the sons of Rameses III on the list at Medinet Habu (*L.D.*, III, 214). The facts on which he relied were the great resemblance in structure and plan between the tombs of Rameses Nefer-kau-ra and this tomb, the stucco used being similar, and the same texts being found in both.

He pointed out that Mentuherkhepshef is six on the list of Rameses III, whilst in his tomb he is called "Eldest son of His Majesty" and "Crown Prince." From these facts he considered that the Mentuherkhepshef of the tomb is the eldest son of Rameses Nefer-kau-ra. This theory receives the strongest possible support from the finding of the name of Rameses Nefer-ka-ra on one of the paintings in the tomb.

The probable meaning of this cartouche is that the tomb was painted during the reign of Rameses Nefer-kau-ra, and that, therefore, the prince died in that reign. He is given the title of "Eldest son of His Majesty" and "Crown Prince," and "His Majesty" can refer to no one else but the reigning monarch.

CATALOGUE OF JEWELS AND PRECIOUS OBJECTS FOUND IN THE FUNERARY DEPOSIT OF SETUÎ II AND TAUOSRÎT.

1. **Gold Crown,** weighing 92 grammes, formed of a narrow band, 4 millimetres in breadth, and 0 m ·175 in diameter. The circle is pierced at irregular intervals, varying from 25 to 43 millimetres, with sixteen holes, employed for attaching ornaments in the form of flowers, of which fourteen have been found. The flowers are made in two pieces. The corolla, which measures 3 centimetres in diameter, and is slightly concave, is composed of ten petals, hollow in the centre and soldered at the edges, with rounded tips ; it is stamped out of gold foil. Four of the petals bear the royal cartouches ; two of them, separated by another, which is uninscribed, present the nomen [cartouche], and the prenomen [cartouche] of Setuî II. The petals opposite these have the name of Queen Tauosrît [cartouche] facing the opposite way.

    Behind the corolla is a round-headed knob, 21 millimetres in diameter, which represents the mass of pistils. To this is attached a ring intended to hold the metal wire that fastened the rosette to the crown ; as this ring is larger than the hole, it cannot have fitted into it, and the flowers, therefore, must have been movable when attached to the crown.

    Plate—Gold Diadem of Queen Tauosrît. Flowers as found : Coloured Plate—Rings and Ornaments, Gold Bracelets and Ornaments.

EAR ORNAMENTS.

2. **Pair of gold Ear-pendants,** composed of two principal parts. The upper part is in two pieces, each formed of a disc, with a tube fixed to the centre of the under side. The two tubes are striated and fit into each other, maintaining an interval of 31 millimetres

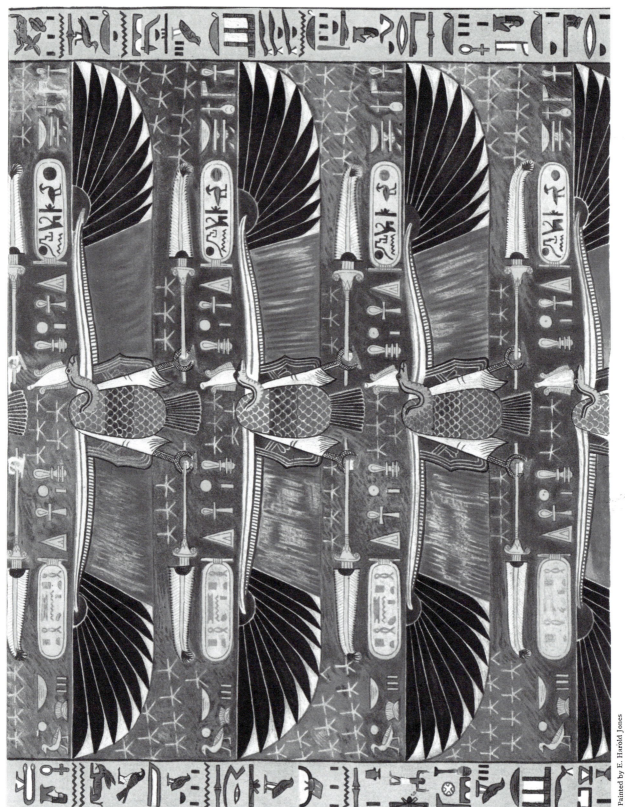

CEILING IN MAIN CORRIDOR

Painted by E. Harold Jones

Painted by E. Harold Jones

ISIS

FRAGMENT OF MUD WITH GOLD BEADS IN POSITION

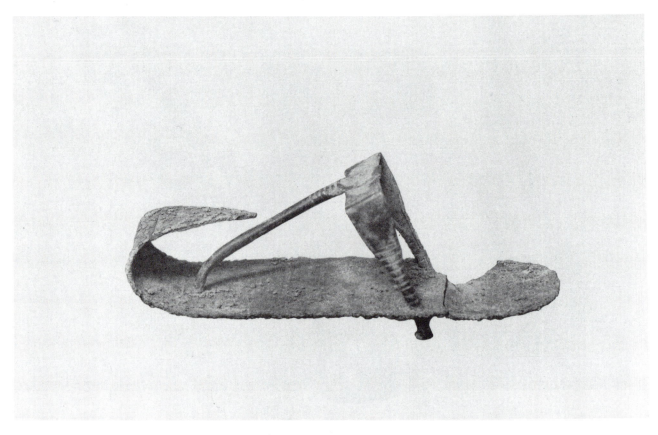

SILVER SANDAL

VASE OF ALABASTER

VASE OF GLAZED FAIENCE WITH
CARTOUCHES OF SETUÎ II

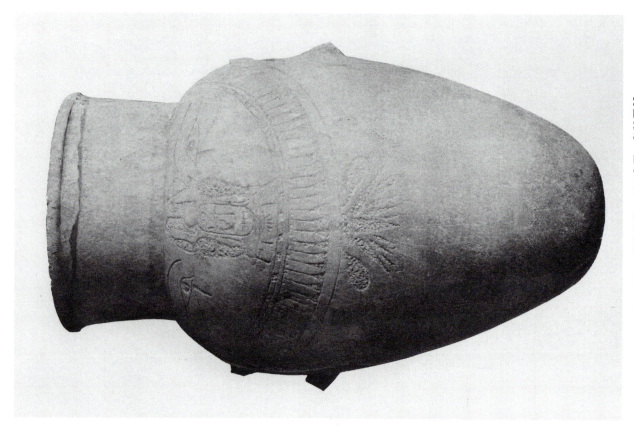

ALABASTER VASE WITH
CARTOUCHE OF RAMESES II

ALABASTER VASE WITH
CARTOUCHE OF RAMESES II

PRINCE MENTUHERKHEPSHEF.

DOG AND MONKEY, FROM TOMB No. 50.

EXCAVATIONS

IN THE

TOMBS OF THE KINGS.

CONTENTS.

PREFACE.

I DESIRE to express my gratitude to Dr. Professor Schafer, of Berlin, for allowing me to publish the beautiful "Head of an Unknown Queen."

THEODORE M. DAVIS.

NEWPORT,
RHODE ISLAND,
U.S.A.

LIST OF ILLUSTRATIONS.

2

A SKETCH OF QUEEN TÎYI'S LIFE.

A SKETCH OF QUEEN TÎYI'S LIFE.

BY G. MASPERO.

§ I.—IS THE NEW PLACE THE TOMB OF TÎYI, OR OF KHUNIATONU?

FIRST of all it must be clearly understood that the vault discovered by Davis is not a real tomb; it is a rough cell in the rock, which has been used as a secret burying-place for a member of the family of the so-called Hæretic Kings, when the reaction in favour of Amon triumphed. The transfer of the mummy from its original tomb at Thebes, or El-Amarna, was devised and made in order to save it from the wrath of victorious sectarians; if this had not been the case, it would have been destroyed or robbed of its treasures. Only two Pharaohs are likely to have been actuated by kind feelings for Khuniatonu—those two who were connected with his family, Aî and Tuatankhamanu—it was one of them who planned and executed the operation. That he succeeded in carrying it out secretly is evident from the fact that, while the Tombs of the Kings were desecrated and plundered completely, this place, with its wealth of gold, remained concealed and untouched until last year. The whole furniture was still in it, ready to bear witness as to the name and rank of its owner.

When subsequently tested, its evidence was both obscure and conflicting. Such of the small objects as were inscribed bore the name of Amenôthes III and of his wife Tîyi, proving that the set of tiny pots, boxes, tools, fictitious offerings, in enamelled stone or glazed pottery, were the property of the queen. The big catafalque, in which the body had been borne to its resting-place on the day of the burial, belonged to the same lady, and its inscriptions state that King Khuniatonu ⌖, "had "made it for the king's mother, great wife of the king, Tîyi." So far, so good, and there seemed to be no possible ground for doubting that the tomb was Tîyi's; but when we came to examine the mosaic coffin and the sheets of gold in which the mummy was wrapped, we found that their legends asserted the mummy to be no other than Khuniatonu himself. It was very badly preserved, having been soaked in water and partly crushed by a block which had fallen from the roof, so that what remained of it was little more than disconnected bones, with a few shreds of dried skin and flesh adhering to or hanging from them. Dr. Elliot Smith, who studied the skull minutely, pronounced it to be the skull of a man aged about twenty-five or twenty-six years. Whether or not he be right about the age is a matter for anatomists only to decide; there is evidence, however, that the body discovered in Davis's vault is that of a man, and that man Khuniatonu, if we must accept the testimony of the inscriptions.

Such being the facts, how are we to reconcile them and explain satisfactorily the presence of Khuniatonu's body amidst Tîyi's furniture? This paradoxical combination may either have been made on purpose, or be the result of some mistake on the part of the persons who executed the transfer. In the first case, we ought, perhaps, to conjecture that, wishing to prevent any harm being done to the king by some fanatical devotee of Amon, the hiders wanted the people to believe that the body they were burying was Tîyi's: accordingly, they took with it Tîyi's catafalque and Tîyi's small furniture, the only exception being the canopic jars which, from the shape of the face, I assume to have been Khuniatonu's. I must confess that I look on this explanation as being too far-fetched to hold good. The second supposition seems to me to be nearer the truth: the mummies of the dead members of Khuniatonu's family must have been taken out of their tombs and brought over to Thebes all together, with such articles of their furniture as it was thought they needed most. Once there, they must have been kept quietly for a few days in some remote chapel of the Necropolis, as were the mummies of Setuî I and other Pharaohs before reaching their last retreat at Deir el-Bahari. When the time came for each to be taken to the hiding-place which had been prepared for them in the Bibân el-Molûk, the men who had charge of these secret funerals mixed the coffins, and put the son where the mother ought to have been. Visitors to the Cairo Museum, who have seen the coffins of Iouîya and Touîyou, and how like they are to each other, will not wonder at such a confusion having been made, especially if we suppose that the transfer took place at night time.

I believe that Davis's vault was originally designed for Tîyi, and for Tîyi's furniture, but that Khuniatonu's mummy was buried in it by mistake. There is still some chance that Khuniatonu's appointed tomb may be discovered in the Bibân el-Molûk with Tîyi's mummy lying in state amongst her son's property

§ II.—THE FACTS ABOUT TÎYI.

The name ⟨hieroglyphs⟩ is read sometimes Thïy : even if it were proved that the sign ⟨hieroglyph⟩ was pronounced commonly *th* in the language of the second Theban Empire, the syllabic ⟨hieroglyph⟩ has for its equivalent ⟨hieroglyphs⟩ ⟨hieroglyphs⟩ with a ⟨hieroglyph⟩ *t*, and not a ⟨hieroglyph⟩. The pronunciation Tîyi, or with the dialectal ᴇ, Têye, is the right one, and is supported by the testimony of the Assyrian monuments.

Tîyi was a daughter of Iouîya and Touîyou, his wife, both of whom were Egyptians of mediocre, if not of low, extraction.[1] Iouîya seems to have been originally a member of the priesthood of Minu, lord of Akhmîm, a prophet of that god ⟨hieroglyphs⟩, and a superintendent of his herds of oxen ⟨hieroglyphs⟩. Touîyou was a "Chauntress of Amanu" ⟨hieroglyphs⟩ "and a tire-woman of the king" ⟨hieroglyphs⟩, not, as it has been said, "the "Mistress of the robes," but one of the women who kept the robes of the king in order, and who helped to dress him every day. The higher titles and epithets, which we find affixed to their names on their own coffins and funerary furniture, were given to them in after life, when their daughter was queen of Egypt.

There are a few dated monuments of Tîyi's life, scarabs for the most part. Perhaps the most important of them is that one which records the Wild Cattle Hunt, not so much on account of the facts on it, but because it has a date of the second year of Amenôthes's reign :—

⟨hieroglyphic inscription⟩

"The IInd year, under the Majesty of King Amenôthes III, and the Great
"Wife of the King, Tîyi, living like Raîya."[2]

---

[1] See Davis, *The Tomb of Iouîya and Touîyou*, pp. xiii–xxiv.

[2] Two specimens of these scarabs are known : the first belonged to Mr. G. W. Frazer, and was published by him in the *Proceedings*, t. XXI, Pl. III, pp. 155, 156, and in the *Catalogue* of his collection of scarabs, Pl. XVI and p. 56 ; the second belonged to the Rev. W. MacGregor, and was published by Newberry, *Scarabs*, Pl. XXXIII, 1, and pp. 173–176.

The form of the date proves that the indication of the second year applies as much to her as to her husband, as she was already a queen at that early date. After this second year, there are no dated monuments of her until we come to the tenth year, and then two scarabs were issued, one recording the number of lions which the king had killed with his own hand :—

"King Amenôthes III and Queen Tîyi, living . . . from the first year until "the year 10 . ."[1]

while the second refers to the coming to Egypt of Giloukhipa, daughter of Shoutarna, king of Mitani :—

"Year 10, under the Majesty of King Amenôthes III and Queen Tîyi, living, "whose father's name is Iouîya, and whose mother's name is Touîyou."

The last date in the combined reign of Amenôthes and Tîyi is that of the eleventh year, and is to be found on a scarab which relates the inauguration of an artificial lake in the city of Zaloukha :—[3]

---

[1] About forty specimens of this scarab are known, for an account of which I refer to Newberry, *Scarabs*, Pl. XXXII, 2, and p. 171.

[2] Two copies of it are known, one in the Berlin Museum, the other in the possession of Baroness Hoffmann ; *cf.* Newberry, *Scarabs*, Pl. XXXII, 1, and p. 170.

[3] This name, which had been correctly read by the first Egyptologists up to the time of Wiedemann (*Aegyptische Geschichte*, p. 382), was miscorrected into Zalou-Selle of the Delta; the true reading has been restored lately by Steindorff and Breasted (*Zeitschrift*, 1901, pp. 62–66).

"Year 11, third month of Akhaît, the first, under the Majesty of King
  "Amenôthes III and Queen Tîyi, living.—His Majesty ordered a lake
  "to be made for Queen Tîyi, living, in her town of Zaloukha, 3,700
  "cubits in length, 700 cubits in breadth. His Majesty made the
  "[usual] feast for the opening of the lakes, in the third month of
  "Akhaît, the sixteenth, when His Majesty sailed upon it in the royal
  "barge *Atontahunu*."

The town of Zaloukha is otherwise unknown, but Steindorff, Breasted,
and Newberry all came independently to the conclusion that it was identical
with the palace-town of Amenôthes III and Tîyi, which was discovered by
Grébaut and partly excavated by Tytus six years ago : the lake which the
king made for his wife would be the modern Birket Habou. Even conceding
that the so-called Birket Habou is the site of an old reservoir—which has
never been proved—the difference between its dimensions and the measure-
ments on the scarab is so great, that it is difficult to admit the proposed
identification.

From this eleventh year to the end of the reign we possess no dated record
of Tîyi but one document, and this, though bearing no mention of a regnal
year, refers to an event which happened, at the latest, in the first year. This
is the so-called Marriage scarab : [2]

"King Amenôthes III and Queen Tîyi, living, whose father's name is Iouîya
  "and whose mother's name is Touîyou, and who is the wife of the
  "strong king, whose southern boundary is to Kalaî, and the northern is
  "to Naharaina." [3]

---

[1] With reference to the four specimens of this scarab which are known, *cf.* Newberry, *Scarabs*,
Pl. XXXIII, 2, and pp. 176–178.

[2] Newberry, *Scarabs*, Pl. XXXII, 3, and p. 172.

[3] Breasted, *Antient Records of Egypt*, t. II, pp. 344, 345, and *A History of Egypt*, pp. 329, 330.

The conclusion that this scarab was issued in remembrance of the marriage has been drawn from the insistence with which Amenôthes says that " the " Great Wife of the king, Tîyi . . . . she is the wife of the strong king." It seems to me, however, that the real meaning of the inscription is to be elicited, not from that part of the inscription, but from the last words, in which the limits of the empire are indicated : they assert the power of Amenôthes and the extent of his dominions in such a way, that they lead us to suppose that the scarab was destined to proclaim the accession of a new king. I should therefore see in it an Accession, and not a Marriage, scarab. The reason why the king put so much stress on the fact that Tîyi was his wife, is probably to be sought for in the departure from traditional customs which he made when he inserted her name in the official protocol : no queen had been thus honoured before his time. If this interpretation prevailed, it would confirm us in the opinion that Amenôthes married Tîyi while he was still heir to the crown.[1]

Those are all the dated facts in the united lives of Amenôthes III and Tîyi ; the undated are not so scarce, and they bear witness to the powerful influence which Tîyi exerted on her husband. She acted with him in the ceremonies for the consecration of the temples he restored or built. Thus, at Soleb, in Nubia, where Amenôthes was associated with the cult of Amon-ra, she followed him with her sons and daughters, and she made homage to his deity ;[2] to show his gratitude, he built a temple for her, at Sedeinga, of which temple she was the Goddess.[3] In Egypt itself she appears next to him on the famous Memnon Colossi at Thebes, and on numerous small objects, lists of which are to be found in recent books on the history of Egypt ;[4] we learn from them nothing more than what we knew already from other sources. The only monument which is of interest for us is the large group from Medinet Habu, now transferred to the Cairo Museum :[5] there we see her sitting next to her husband, and with them three of their daughters :

Nabîtâhâou, and a third one, whose

Honîttaunebu, and a third one, whose

---

[1] Breasted, *A History of Egypt*, p. 329, admits the possibility of his having married Tîyi " already as crown prince."

[2] Cailliaud, *Voyage à Méroé*, Atlas, t. II, Pl. 14 ; Lepsius, *Denkmäler*, III, Pl. 83–88.

[3] Lepsius, *Denkmäler*, III, Pl. 82, *e–i*.

[4] Wiedemann, *Aegyptische Geschichte*, pp. 389–392 ; Flinders Petrie, *A History of Egypt*, t. II, pp. 202, 203.

[5] Daressy, *Notes et Remarques*, § CCII, in *Recueil de Travaux*, t. XXIV, pp. 165, 166.

name has completely disappeared. Honîttaunebu is probably identical with the ⸢[hieroglyphs]⸣, who, according to Lepsius, was represented in the temple at Soleb.[1] The group is in the best Theban style of the period, with idealized features : the face of the queen is rounded and regular, and bears very little resemblance to her real face as it is known to us from the head found by Petrie in Sinai.

Tîyi bore many children to Amenôthes III, only five of whom are known to us, four daughters, [hieroglyphs] Isît,[2] [hieroglyphs] Honîttaunebu, transcribed in error [hieroglyphs] Honitmerhabi,[3] [hieroglyphs] Sîtamanu who was probably the third daughter in the group in the Cairo Museum,[4] [hieroglyphs] Bakîtniatonu, of whom more anon, and a son who was afterwards the celebrated Amenôthes V—Khuniatonu. Nothing but the name is known concerning the three eldest daughters, and the place of the fourth in the family was misunderstood until quite recently. As she appears only at El-Amarna, and bears a name composed with Atonu, she was supposed to be a daughter of Khuniatonu. Now we have proof that she was Tîyi's daughter, born, probably, somewhat late in the reign of Amenôthes III.[5] The original form of her name may have been [hieroglyphs] Bakîtniamanu, and the final Amanu changed to Atonu during her brother's reign ; this, however, is mere conjecture. She must have been quite young when her father died, for she is represented as a girl in the twelfth year of Khuniatonu, and was unmarried at that time. As none of the three eldest sisters are alluded to under Khuniatonu, it seems probable that they died in their father's lifetime.

When her son came to power, Tîyi continued at first to enjoy great authority. The king of Mitani, Dushratta, wrote directly to her and implored her to exert her influence with her son, to obtain for him certain favours, or according to his view rights, he was claiming, and whenever he

---

[1] Lepsius, *Denkmäler*, III, Pl. 86*b* ; *cf.* Lepsius, *Königsbuch*, no. 379, and Bouriant-Brugsch, *Le Livre des Rois*, no. 356.

[2] Lepsius, *Denkmäler*, III, Pl. 86*b* ; *cf.* Brugsch-Bouriant, *Le Livre des Rois*, no. 356.

[3] Flinders Petrie, *Illahun*, Pl. XVII, no. 20 ; Daressy, *Notes et Remarques*, § CCII, in *Recueil de Travaux*, t. XXIV, pp. 165, 166 and under the faulty form, Lepsius, *Denkmäler*, III, Pl. 86*b*.

[4] Birch, in *Archaeological Journal*, t. VIII, p. 297 ; Mariette, *Abydos*, t. II, Pl. 49 ; Flinders Petrie, *Tell el-Amarna*, Pl. XIII, no. 16 ; Dr. DAVIS, *The Tomb of Iouîya*, pp. 38, 43.

[5] Flinders Petrie, *A History of Egypt*, t. II, pp. 203, 204 ; N. de G. Davis, *The Rock Tombs of El-Amarna*, t. III, Pl. XVIII, and pp. 15, 16,

wrote to Khuniatonu, he adjured him to consult his mother about the friendly relations he had entertained with her husband. [1] Nevertheless, it seems that after a time she was, if not put completely aside, at least left out of most political affairs. She is never mentioned in the documents in which Khuniatonu narrates how he founded his new capital and inaugurated or enlarged it ; only his wife, Nofrîteîti, and her daughters are represented as participating with the king in the rites of consecration. Is this a sufficient reason to allow us to affirm that, though she had a palace in El-Amarna[2] and a household, of which a certain Houîya was a superintendent,[3] she did not reside there habitually, but that she lived, most of her time, in her palace at Thebes ? It needs more proofs than we have to make such an assertion, and to draw from it the conclusion that, far from being the inspirer of the Atonian creed, she preferred to keep out of it as far as it was compatible with her dignity of mother of the reformer. One thing only is certain, that is, that about the twelfth year of her son's reign ⌈𓂋𓈖𓇳𓅱𓏪𓇋𓏏𓏏𓈖𓇳𓏪⌉,[4] she was in El-Amarna. I say *about* the twelfth year, because the date relates, not to any fact in which she was necessarily concerned, but to a reception by the king of Syrian and Ethiopian tributes, and Tîyi's visit might have occurred somewhat earlier or somewhat later. The different episodes of her stay are depicted freely in Houîya's tomb. A tableau is dedicated to the memory of her husband, and associates him with the honours she is receiving from her son. Amenôthes III sits on a chair in front of his royal wife, and raises his own hand towards one of the small hands with which the rays of the sun are provided. Her protocol is written behind her :

" The Princess, the most praised, the lady of grace, sweet in her love, who fills
    " the palace with her beauties, the Regent of the South and the North,
    " the great wife of the king who loves him, the lady of both lands, Tîyi,"

exactly as if her husband was still living. In front of her, her youngest daughter, Bakîtatonu , raises her hand

---

[1] Winckler, *Die Thontafeln von Tell el-Amarna*, pp. 68–81.

[2] Flinders Petrie, *Tell-Amarna*, Pl. XXII, and p. 33.

[3] See his titles in N. de G. Davis, *The Rock Tombs of El-Amarna*, t. III, Pl. I–XXV, and pp. 1–25.

[4] N. de G. Davies, *The Rock Tombs of El-Amarna*, t. III, Pl. XIII, p. 9.

towards her father.[1]   In another place we see how she was invited to the table of the king, and how she sat in front of her son and of her daughter-in-law with Bakîtatonu ; she is crowned with the diadem of the two feathers and the sun-disk on flaming horns, while Pharaoh and his wife wear an ordinary head-dress.[2]   The entertainment was protracted till late into the night, and ended in a kind of drinking bout,[3] as in some of the tales in the *Arabian Nights*.   Further on, it is shown how she was led by her son to the temple of Atonu,[4] where a part of the building was known as the *Sun-shade of Tîyi*, in parallelism with the *Sun-shade* ⌐ of her son.[5]

Thus she disappears from our eyes in a kind of apotheosis.

§ III.—CONCLUSION.

When we come to examine coolly the few facts which are known about Tîyi, very little remains of the romance with which most early writers have surrounded her person.   She was an Egyptian, born of parents of low, or, at the best, of middle condition, and her father was in the service of a provincial Egyptian god.   She was already married to Amenôthes when he notified officially his accession to the throne, and she was invested by her husband with the full honours of a reigning queen of Egypt.   Her fame passed the frontiers of Egypt, and the vassal or allied kings of Asia tried to win her goodwill whenever they were in need of help, or when they claimed a gift from their liege.   Her power lasted till the death of Amenôthes III and continued for awhile under Amenôthes IV, but she probably remained in Thebes and came to Khuniatonu occasionally ; her last visit was about the twelfth year of her son's reign.   It seems probable that she died in his lifetime.   Whether she was buried at Thebes or at El-Amarna, we are not able to say.   I have already given above, in Section I of this sketch, a possible explanation of the facts connected with the presence of part of her funerary apparel in the hiding place at Bibân el-Molûk.

Milon-la-Chapelle,
        22nd September, 1908.

---

[1] N. de G. Davies, *The Rock Tombs of El-Amarna*, t. III, Pl. XVIII, and pp. 15, 16.
[2] *Ibid.*, t. III, Pl. IV, V, and pp. 4–7.
[3] *Ibid.*, t. III, Pl. VI, VII, and p. 7.
[4] *Ibid.*, t. III, Pl. VII–XII, and pp. 7–9.
[5] On this *Sunshade*, *cf.* N. de G. Davies, *The Rock Tombs of El-Amarna*, t. III, pp. 19–25.

A NOTE ON THE ESTIMATE OF THE AGE ATTAINED BY THE PERSON WHOSE SKELETON WAS FOUND IN THE TOMB.

BY

G. ELLIOT SMITH, M.A., M.D., F.R.S.,

Professor of Anatomy in the Egyptian Government School of Medicine, Cairo:
sometime Fellow of St. John's College, Cambridge.

WHEN these bones were sent to me for examination two years ago, I reported that they formed the greater part of the skeleton of a young man, who, judged by the ordinary European standards of ossification, must have attained an age of about twenty-five or twenty-six years at the time of his death. At the same time I called attention to the fact that the dates at which the various bones of the human skeleton underwent consolidation and ceased growing were subject to a very wide range of variation in different individuals, so that a bone which had reached its full development in one person at twenty years of age might, in another, be still incomplete at twenty-five, and a vertebra, which might be complete at twenty-five years of age in one man, may take five years longer to become consolidated in another person.

Such considerations led me to make the reservation that the estimated age of twenty-five or twenty-six years might, in any given individual, be lessened or increased by two or three years, if his growth was precocious or delayed, respectively. The question has been put to me by archaeologists: "Is it possible that these bones can be those of a man of twenty-eight or thirty years of age?" For the reasons indicated above, no anatomist would be justified in denying that this individual may have been twenty-eight, but it is highly improbable that he could have attained thirty years if he had been normal.

The cranium, however, exhibits in an unmistakable manner the distortion characteristic of a condition of hydrocephalus. The bones, therefore, cannot be regarded as those of a perfectly normal person, so that there is the possibility—though it is nothing more—that the process of ossification may not have followed the usual course, but have been delayed.

To make this position clear would need a somewhat detailed examination of the technical evidence, which Mr. Davis tells me he does not want for the purposes of this volume.

All that I need state here at present is that, taking the evidence of such standard authorities as POIRIER (PAUL POIRIER ET A. CHARPY, *Traité d'Anatomie Humaine*," Tome I^{ier}, 1899) and TESTUT (*Traité d'Anatomie Humaine*," 1899), and examining it in the light of the data regarding the relation of the times of consolidation of various bones, the one to the other, in a large series of ancient Egyptian skeletons, I still maintain the opinion mentioned above :—that the skeleton is that of a man of twenty-five or twenty-six years of age, without excluding the possibility that he may have been several years older.

GRAFTON ELLIOT SMITH.

THE FINDING OF THE TOMB OF QUEEN TÎYI.

THEODORE M. DAVIS.

On the 1st of January, 1907, having exhausted the surrounding sites, I had to face a space of about forty feet oblong and at least fifty feet high, covered with limestone chippings, evidently the dumping of the surrounding tombs. Within a few feet was the open tomb of Rameses IX, and on the east and south sides were the open tombs of Seti I, and Rameses I, II, and III ; all of which had contributed to the hill. There was no sign of the probability of a tomb. On the contrary, it seemed to be a hopeless excavation, resulting in a waste of time and money. Nevertheless, it had to be cleared, whatever the result. Possibly it may interest the reader to know that the most difficult, delaying, and expensive work is the finding of a place where the débris can be dumped. Generally, it has to be moved two or three times, as the first dumping-ground may probably cover some tomb, therefore the débris must be returned to the original spot, in case no tomb is found.

With a large gang of men, we commenced clearing on the apex of the hill, within a few feet of the tomb of Rameses IX. In the course of a few days we reached the level of the door of his tomb, finding nothing but the chippings of the surrounding tombs. But down we went some thirty feet, when we found stone steps evidently leading to a tomb. Finally, we discovered the lintel of a door which proved to be about eight feet high and six feet wide. It had been closed with large and small stones, held in place with cement or plaster, but, with the exception of a wall about three feet high, these had been pulled down. The clearing of the door, so that we could enter, was soon done, when we found that within a few feet of the door, the mouth of the tomb was filled with stones to within four feet of the roof. On this pile of stones were lying two wooden doors, on each of which copper hinges were fixed. The upper faces of the doors were covered with gold foil marked with the *name and titles of Queen Tîyi*. It is quite

4

impossible to describe the surprise and joy of finding the tomb of the great queen and her household gods, which for these 3,000 years had never been discovered.

The next and most difficult task was to pass the "doors," as they filled the space between the walls and could not be moved for fear of injuring the gold inscriptions. However, with the skill of the native captain, we got a beam about ten inches wide between one wall and the golden door. On this beam I managed to crawl over, striking my head and most of my body but without damaging the doors. I then made my way down the tomb, finding some stones and sand. En route, we noticed many small objects. Within seventy feet we came to a break in the corridor about six feet deep, which proved to be a room about fifteen by eighteen feet, whose walls and roof had been badly cemented. To the right, some five feet from the floor, was a cutting in the rock, about four feet square and three feet high, and in it were four canopic jars with the heads on ; these bore no hieroglyphs and no signs of the original owner.

On the floor near by lay the coffin made of wood, but entirely covered with gold foil and inlaid with semi-precious stones, as will be seen from the photograph in the catalogue. Evidently the coffin had either been dropped or had fallen from some height, for the side had burst, exposing the head and neck of the mummy. On the head plainly appeared a gold crown, encircling the head, as doubtless it was worn in life by a probable queen. Presently we cleared the mummy from the coffin, and found that it was a smallish person, with a delicate head and hands. The mouth was partly open, showing a perfect set of upper and lower teeth. The body was enclosed in mummy-cloth of fine texture, but all of the cloth covering the body was of a very dark colour. Naturally it ought to be a much brighter colour. Rather suspecting injury from the evident dampness, I gently touched one of the front teeth (3,000 years old), and alas ! it fell into dust, thereby showing that the mummy could not be preserved. We then cleared the entire mummy, and found that from the clasped hands to the feet, the body was covered with pure gold sheets, called gold foil, but nearly all so thick that when taken in the hands, they would stand alone without bending. These sheets covered the body from side to side. When we had taken off the gold on the front of the mummy, we lifted it so as to get the gold underneath, which was plainly in sight. Mr. Joseph Lindon Smith, an artist drawing for me, put his hands under a large sheet of gold, and, as he lifted it up, exclaimed : "I have something on my hands which you have never found before." When he gave it to me, I put my hands under it and found them wet with water.

It may be interesting to know how the water got into the tomb and why it remained there. There was a narrow crack in the rock roof within ten feet of the door of the tomb, which I noticed had been originally cemented, evidently as protection against the rain. There was very near it a crack not wider than a knitting-needle, extending six or eight feet. Doubtless, it was supposed that no water could get in there, but it proved not to be so. Probably for many years the water had percolated through the crack and had run down the steep stone floor to the chamber where the mummy lay on the ground. It must be understood that the tomb was absolutely airless, except for what was originally shut in, and what possibly came through the "needle" crack, which after some years was hermetically closed by the dumpings from the numerous surrounding tombs. The air had absorbed all the dampness that it could from the objects in the tomb, but had not the power to absorb the water underneath the body. (In the Iouîya and Touîyou tomb I found a large open alabaster jar, two-thirds full of liquid, probably natron.)

We then took off the gold crown, and attempted to remove the mummy-cloth in which the body was wrapped, but the moment I attempted to lift a bit of the wrapping, it came off in a black mass, exposing the ribs. We then found a beautiful necklace, which is now in the Cairo Museum. It was around the neck and resting on the breast beneath the mummy-cloth.

Subsequently the wrappings of the mummy were entirely removed, exposing the bones. Thereupon, I concluded to have them examined and reported upon by two surgeons who happened to be in the "Valley of the Kings." They kindly made the examination and reported that the pelvis was evidently that of a woman. Therefore, everyone interested in the question accepted the sex, and supposed that the body was doubtless that of Queen Tîyi. Some time thereafter, the bones were sent to Dr. G. Elliot Smith, Professor of Anatomy in the Egyptian Government School of Medicine, Cairo, for his inspection and decision. Alas! Dr. Smith declared the sex to be male. It is only fair to state that the surgeons were deceived by the abnormal pelvis and the conditions of the examination.

Within a few feet of the coffin, the four alabaster canopic jars were standing in a small excavation in the stone wall. The heads were on the jars, but, on examination, it proved that the ordinary contents had been removed before the jars had been deposited in the tomb. There had been inscriptions on each vase, but for some unknown reason they had been carefully obliterated, but the "sky" sign clearly shows on every jar.

There have been some suggestions that the heads are portraits of Khuniatonu (Amenhotep IV). It seems to me to be certain that if the heads were his, they would have been extremely elongated as was his usual practice. In evidence of this, it will be seen on a plaque which Khuniatonu caused to be made of wood, covered with gold foil, whereon is Tîyi's portrait, he represented her head and face elongated in his usual style (see Plates 29–33). From these and other evidences, I venture to insist that the beautiful canopic heads are portraits of Queen Tîyi.

There were many very interesting objects in the tomb which I have not mentioned, but by reference to the admirable catalogue of objects made by M. George Daressy, the reader can understand the interest of the find.

In all probability her mummy was buried in a tomb in Tell el-Amarna, and probably would have remained there, but owing to the danger of the destruction of her body during the disturbances after the death of her son, Tut-ank-Amon, the son-in-law of Khuniatonu, doubtless brought the mummy and all the objects theretofore described, and took possession of the tomb. This we know because I found in the tomb several lead seals with his name recorded. No one seems to know why the contents of the tomb were not stolen or destroyed when they reached the tomb in the Valley; nor can one understand why the gold crown at least was not taken by the priests or the workmen.

The tomb in which Tîyi's objects were found was not excavated for her, as M. Maspero says, nevertheless it was not disturbed until I found it. It seems reasonable to suppose that it was so insignificant that it was allowed to remain undisturbed. In addition to this, the makers of the surrounding tombs treated the site as a barren place to dump the rocks from the various tombs, thereby protecting Tîyi's deposit. We all know that insignificance spares many people from various troubles, as was the case with Tîyi and with Iouîya and Touîyou.

A short time ago, I found a small pit tomb about three hundred feet from Tîyi's tomb. It was covered with rock and sand about three feet deep. It proved to be about seven feet square and six feet deep. It was filled with white jars sealed with covers. We opened them and found that one contained various interesting objects pertaining to burials. The remainder of the jars contained small red cups, many square limestone blocks, fairly well polished, and many other objects of little value, etc. Evidently they came from a poor man's tomb, from which the contents were carefully removed and secreted in the pit tomb I have described. In all probability the contents were removed for the purpose of finding a tomb for Queen Tiyi. The poverty of the style of the tomb suggests that it was the only one that could be found in the vicinity. In any event, it seems that the selection of this tomb probably protected the deposits from robbery.

I have recently found in one of the jars a bundle of mummy-cloth which had been used for the protection of some of the fragile objects. On spreading it there appeared hieroglyphics reading, "Good God, lord of Egypt, loved by Min. Year 6th." It therefore is certain that he directed the clearing of the tomb of all its contents, which he deposited in the Pit-tomb, and then took possession of the tomb wherein he deposited all the objects of Queen Tîyi.

THE EXCAVATION OF THE TOMB OF QUEEN TÎYI, 1907.

EDWARD R. AYRTON.

THE central point and the meeting place of all the Wadis at the southern end of the Valley of the Tombs of the Kings at Thebes is occupied by a large rock mound, in which Rameses IX excavated a great tomb for himself, running into the western face ; and various smaller tombs have been discovered to the north of his sepulchre on the western and northern sides of the mound. The western face to the south of the tomb was, however, covered with an immense heap of limestone chips thrown out by the masons engaged in cutting the tomb of Rameses VI which lies opposite, and, as this had never been touched in more recent times, we removed the greater part in the hopes of finding some older tomb of importance beneath. After sinking deep pits and trenches down the side of the rock face, we had almost given up hope when we came across several large jars of the XXth dynasty type lying together in what appeared to be a recess in the rock. On digging deeper we came to a cut face with squared corners on either side, showing that a tomb had at least been begun at this spot. We then sunk a pit straight down through the chippings, which at this depth were cemented together by the action of water, until we came to a layer of clean dry limestone fragments which led us to hope that the tomb might have escaped the fate of that of Siphtah which we had found so damaged by the entrance of water. Below this clean rubbish we struck a flight of well-cut stone steps and knew that we had discovered a tomb of the XVIIIth dynasty and no mere burial pit.

Turning on our full gang of men we made a thorough clearance down to the entrance of the tomb, which had evidently been begun on a smaller scale and then enlarged. We found the doorway closed by a loosely-built wall of limestone fragments, resting not on the rock beneath, but on the loose rubbish which had filled the stairway. This we removed and found behind it the remains of the original sealing of the door. This was composed of rough blocks of limestone cemented together and coated on the outside with cement of so hard a quality that a knife could scarcely scratch it ; on this we found the impressions of the oval seal of the priestly college of Amon-ra at Thebes— a jackal crouching over nine captives. This wall we also removed and began the clearance of the corridor, which we found filled with rubbish to within some three feet of the ceiling, near the first doorway, and sloping towards the other end until the space from the ceiling was almost six feet. This rubbish consisted of clean limestone chippings which gave the appearance of never having been moved far from the tomb or left outside for any length of time. Lying on this rubbish, at a few feet from the door by which we had entered, lay a large wooden object resembling a broad sled in shape. It was covered with gold-leaf with a line of inscription running down each side. On it lay a wooden door with copper pivots still in place ; this also was covered with gold-leaf and ornamented with a scene in low relief of a queen worshipping the Sun-disk. On both of the objects lay fragments of limestone which had injured the gold. When we examined the gold we discovered the cartouche of the famous Queen Tîyi. Our workmen succeeded in improvising a bridge consisting of a narrow beam without injury to the gold. We crawled along this narrow bridge and over the rubbish beyond we came to a second doorway which was more or less clear of rubbish. From the sill we clambered down a long broad slope of chippings and débris into a large oblong room, the walls of which were coated with stucco, but undecorated. The interior seemed to be in a state of complete confusion. On the slope down which we had just come lay a wooden door exactly similar to that which we had found in the corridor, and beside it stood a large alabaster vase-stand. Against the opposite wall of the room were leaning what appeared to be the sides and cornice of an enormous casket-shaped box. On the ground to the left lay another side of apparently the same box, whilst square beams lay scattered about the floor. Wherever the woodwork lay horizontally the stucco and gold-leaf still adhered and the scenes and inscriptions on them were consequently preserved ; but of the pieces leaning against the wall, only one still retained part of its original decoration. In the further corners lay the remains of small wooden boxes, and in a small chamber or recess in the right-hand wall one could distinguish the four canopic jars. Just beneath the recess there lay a wooden coffin covered with gold-leaf and inlaid with carnelian and glass; it had fallen in on one side exposing the head of the mummy, on which appeared a gold crown.

All the woodwork in the tomb was, however, in so fragile a state that nothing could be touched and it was therefore decided that, besides the usual views of the interior, photographs should be taken of each thing as it stood before we attempted the removal of anything. An expert photographer was telegraphed for from Cairo, and work on the tomb was suspended for a few days until he had taken the desired photographs, since we found that the shifting of rubbish so stirred up the dust as to quite obscure all outline, and would therefore be fatal to photography. The photographing finished, we began the clearance of the corridor. On first entering we had noticed, at a few feet from the door, a long crack in the roof, which had been ineffectually stopped up with cement, through which a certain amount of rain-water had entered the tomb, and it was owing to this accident that the woodwork in the large room was so fragile. The water had had the same effect on the wood in the corridor, and we found that it would be quite impossible to remove it without damaging the designs on the surface. We therefore decided to leave it in position, and this we were able to do by careful underpinning of the whole structure with planks and beams, which enabled us to remove the whole of the rubbish from beneath, leaving it suspended in air.

In the rubbish of the corridor, which we now removed as far as the entrance of the room, were only found a copper graving tool, a wooden mallet head, and a few beads, whilst we found that the old woodwork had been partly upheld at one end by the lid of what must have been a very large alabaster vase. We now had sufficient space to work in and turned our attention to the coffin. The lid had, as we have already noticed, collapsed inwards, splitting into two halves from the feet to the neck; we were consequently able to remove it in three sections, laying each piece as it was removed on a specially prepared padded tray, and each in turn was then carried out and placed in the corridor.

Beneath this lay the remains of the mummy, wrapped in flexible gold plates, but the wrappings had been so affected by moisture that they crumbled to the touch, and the bones would only just bear handling.

Round the neck were the remains of a broad necklace of gold pendants and inlaid plaques connected by rows of minute beads, and ending in large lotus flowers of gold, inlaid with paste. The left arm was bent with the hand on the breast, and round the upper arm were three broad bracelets of very thin gold of a fragile nature; the right arm was laid straight down by

5

the side, the hand resting on the thigh, and remains of three similar bracelets were round the wrist; no rings or other jewellery were found with the mummy.

Under the coffin was a long wooden boarding covered with gold-leaf, at the head of which were found lions' heads in wood, suggesting that the coffin had originally lain on a raised couch, which by collapsing, had let the coffin fall to the ground, and the falling lid had thus broken up the mummy.

After we had moved the canopic jars from the small side-chamber, we started sifting the whole of the rubbish on the floor, and were rewarded by finding numerous small objects.

In the south-west corner were the remains of a large oblong wooden box, which had collapsed under the weight of stucco fallen from the wall above. The wood was, however, in good condition, and we were able to remove it. Between this and the west wall were the remains of another box of small size—which may have originally fitted into the larger—so affected by the moisture that it crumbled to the touch. It had been full of small vases, wands, and figures of blue glazed ware.

Four inscribed mud tablets, on two of which the cartouche of Akhenaten is legible, were found, respectively (*a*) in the north-west corner; (*b*) under the mummy couch; (*c*) in the small side-chamber; and (*d*) against the east wall at about seven feet from the north-east corner.

In the rubbish under the funeral couch and behind the boards against the south wall we found numerous fragments of small clay seals, some of which bore, besides the device, the cartouche of Neb-kheperu-ra (Tutankhamen). The remains of a necklace of small blue beads were found near to the north-east corner scattered about in the rubbish.

CATALOGUE OF THE OBJECTS

FOUND IN THE

TOMB OF QUEEN TÎYI,

BY

GEORGE DARESSY.

I. SEPULCHRAL CANOPY.

1. The Sepulchral Canopy.—The entrance corridor and the sepulchral chamber contained the panels of a great sarcophagus, or, more precisely, of a hearse which must have served to protect the coffin during its transport to the necropolis. The catafalque, of rectangular form, which opened in front with folding-doors, is made of cedar-wood, now rotted by damp; it was covered with stucco, engraved and gilded, but this decoration also is in bad condition and is breaking off in fragments to such an extent that there is no hope of preserving it. Copies made on the spot by Mr. Ayrton enable me to give the following details:

Front. On the upper traverse two inscriptions face each other; left, [hieroglyphs]; right, [hieroglyphs]. (Pl. XXXI.)

Door-posts.—On the posts forming the jambs of the door is a vertical column of hieroglyphs, and the ornament [hieroglyph] at the base. On the left jamb was inscribed[1] [hieroglyphs] [hieroglyphs]. The prenomen of Amenôthes IV had been erased and that of Amenôthes III substituted in red ink.

On the right-hand post: [hieroglyphs]. (Pl. XXXI.)

Door.—One of the leaves of the door was found in the corridor; the other in the chamber. The bronze hinges were still attached to them (*see* No. 3).

On them Queen Tîyi was figured offering flowers to Aten, the rayed disc. The legends engraved above this scene referred, some of them, to the disc: [1][hieroglyphs] [2][hieroglyphs] (below 1 and 2)

[1] As there is no typographical sign in existence representing the [sign] under the Aten disc, the sign ♀ has been substituted therefor.

[hieroglyphs] others to the Queen, [hieroglyphs]

[hieroglyphs]

Back.—Inscription of the upper border twice repeated symmetrically :

[hieroglyphs]

On the left upright : [hieroglyphs];

on the right : [hieroglyphs].

The panel is entirely occupied by a scene of adoration of Aten. (Pl. XXXII.) The disc placed near the left corner emits rays terminating in hands ; some of these receive the offerings, and others protect the king and queen, holding the sign of life to their nostrils. The altar placed below the disc bears six cartouches, those of Aten, twice repeated, and those of the king, which have been erased. Besides what is placed on the altar, there are tables laden with bread and food-products, and amphorae are placed in light wooden stands. The king, the whole of whose figure has been erased, was standing about the middle of the scene, wearing on his head the helmet with two striped ribbons, and holding the baton [glyph] employed to strike objects offered to divinities. Behind him is Queen Tîyi dressed in a long airy robe ; her neck covered with a wide necklace, her head adorned by a wig of small curls ; her forehead is encircled by a crown, in front of which are two uraei with the horns of Isis on their heads ; she is wearing the head-dress of the goddess Hathor, the disc surmounted by two long feathers. The features of the queen are remarkable : she has the long face and prominent chin that characterise the portraits of the reign of Khuniatonu. She seems to be pouring water on the pile of offerings in front of her, out of which flames are apparently issuing. (Pl. XXXIII.)

Inscriptions are engraved above this scene, referring to the disc :

[hieroglyphs]

[hieroglyphs]

or to the king and his mother :

[hieroglyphs]

LARGE PANELS.—The stucco of the lateral panels is in a worse condition than that of the ends. It is only possible to recognise that the scenes on them also are adoration of the rayed disc and the dedication of altars of offerings. (Pl. XXVIII.) The horizontal inscription above the scene reads thus:

2. Bronze Tenons.—Four bronze tenons found among the rubbish served to fasten the cover to the sarcophagus described above. They are roughly rectangular in form, with rounded corners, strips of metal, 6 to 7 millimetres in thickness. Their dimensions, length and breadth, are: A.—0 m ·23 × 0 m ·068; B.—0 m ·21 × 0 m ·065; C.—0 m ·23 × 0 m ·07; D.—0 m ·225 × 0 m ·07. The upper part of the second tenon has been completely severed. It was cut in a straight line through half the thickness of the metal by chisels, and then snapped off by wrenching it sideways. (Pl. XXIII.)

The upper half of the tenons were inserted into the wood of the cover, and fixed there by a bronze peg 0 m ·038 in length: the lower half to a depth of 0 m ·115 fitted into a cavity worked in the thickness of the sarcophagus. On each tenon there is a column of inscription bearing the name and title of Queen Tîyi:

3. Door Hinges.—The folding-doors of the catafalque still retained their two bronze hinges, length 0 m ·13, heights with the pivots 0 m ·25 and 0 m ·09. They consist, as usual, of one piece, hollow and rectangular, that fitted round the edge of the door; its breadth is 0 m ·045, the space between the sides being 0 m ·04: to this is attached a conical pivot in the case of the lower hinge, the upper one has a cylindrical pin. These objects seem to have been covered with gold-leaf, now fallen off as the result of oxydation. On the lintel of the door there was still the hollow bronze cylinder, height 0 m ·04, diameter 0 m ·048, in which the upper hinge of the door revolved.

6.

II. COFFIN.

---

4. Coffin.—The coffin that contained the mummy is the richest and most highly decorated of all that have hitherto been found. Sculptured, gilded, and inlaid, the completion of the various processes employed in its ornamentation must have occupied a considerable length of time. Unfortunately, it has reached us in a very bad state of preservation, the boards disjointed, the wood rotted, the stucco powdering off, and the inlays falling out of their sockets, the result of so many centuries spent in a tomb into which water had penetrated.

The coffin is in cedar-wood, of human form, and consists of two pieces, the receptacle and the cover, held to each other by tenons. Its length is 1 m ·75, its breadth 0 m ·56. The whole represented the king at full length, wrapped in bandages from which emerged the head and the two hands crossed on the breast. There is no part which was not either gilded or inlaid with stones and enamel. (Pl. XXX.)

The face was covered with a gold mask, of moderate thickness. Of this the lower part is missing from below the eyes, which were inlaid ; to the chin was attached a false beard (see no. 6). The head was covered with a wig similar to that on the heads of the canopic vases (see Pl. VII) : the hair is carefully divided into small coils, parted at the top of the head and falling vertically all round, except in front where they are caught back to the sides of the face in five rows laid over each other, each row diminishing in length. At the back they leave the neck uncovered, but they lengthen by degrees, till in front the two points touch the breast. This hair is carved on pieces of ebony inserted in the wood of the coffin, and thinly covered with gold-leaf. On the forehead is a uraeus in bronze gilt, with the body trailed over the head (see no. 5).

The arms are laid on the breast ; the crossed hands are closed and hold the royal emblems, the crozier and whip (see no. 7) ; on the wrists are wide bracelets adorned with plaques of multicoloured glass. For the remainder of the surface, the wooden case was covered with a coating of fine plaster, over which gold-leaf was laid more or less thickly ; but following a traced design the gilding was cut away, the plaster hollowed and the cavities filled with cut stones or with coloured glass moulded to the shape of the cavities to be filled. These inlays were fixed by a blue or green mastic. For this decoration—polychrome upon a gold ground—the effect of which is very good, the artists employed carnelian for the red, glass coloured with metallic salts for the lapis-blue, turquoise-blue and emerald-green, crystal or crystallised gypsum for the white.

The upper part of the breast is concealed by a collar 16 centimetres wide, composed of seven rows of different ornaments arranged in the following order :

1st row.—Inverted semicircles, red, ▽, interspaced with triangles, green, △.

2nd row.—Tongues, white, ⋃.

3rd row.—Disc in relief, gilded except at the top, a segment inlaid, green, ⊖. These alternate with small chess-boards, ten squares in length by five in height. Here gold squares separate others which are successively blue, red, blue, green, blue in the first row. In the lower rows the colours are repeated in the same order, but each time moving on one colour towards the left.

4th row.—Inverted semi-circles, ▽, separated by triangular petals cut in three pieces, △, the top pale blue, the centre red, the base lapis-blue.

5th row.—Pendant flowers, blue, with a red point projecting from the centre of the corolla, ⋀, between them are elongated green triangles, in imitation of folded leaves, ⋃.

6th row.—Small semi-circles, ▽, between which hang blue glass triangles, striped down the length, △.

7th row.—Pendant flowers, composed of a green calyx above, and a spreading corolla below in striated blue glass, △.

The rest of the body is ornamented in accordance with the method of decoration customary at the commencement of the XVIIIth dynasty, and which has caused the Arabs to give to these coffins the name "rishi," or "feathered." But, while the sarcophagi of Amasis, Nefert-ari, and of the Thothmes' have feathers that cover the entire surface, simply engraved on a thin coating of plaster, which was afterwards gilded, here the feathers are inlaid in a variety of colours, and the gold only marks the outlines.

All the feathers point in the direction of the feet; those that cover the bust are small with rounded ends, and are imbricated—height 3 centimetres, width 15 millimetres. Each is formed of three pieces, the top lapis blue, the middle a chevron of turquoise-blue, the base red.

The lower part of the body is decorated according to a different scheme. Down the middle there is an inscription which extends from the arms to the feet. The hieroglyphs, of polychrome inlays, stand out on a plain gold ground, 0 m ·065 wide. On each side of this there are twelve long vertical rows, 2 centimetres wide, in imitation of quills, formed by small plaques of glass arranged in chevrons, successively blue, green, blue, red. The whole of the surface at this level is filled with this scheme of colour.

The column of hieroglyphs between the legs gives the royal titles of Khuniatonu:

On the sides, horizontal bands of inscriptions follow the junction of the coffin and its cover. They repeat the same titles, with one sole variant at the commencement:

The end of the coffin at the foot is covered with gold leaf, on which twelve lines of hieroglyphs are finely engraved, seven upon the cover, five upon the coffin :—

The interior of the coffin was also covered with gold leaf, averaging from 0 m ·42 to 0 m ·20. Down the middle both of the coffin and of the lid there is a single column of hieroglyphs, which were engraved in the wood, and the gold pressed down over it to receive the imprint. These merely give the royal protocol once more, with unimportant variants in the orthography : [hieroglyphs] (coffin [hieroglyphs]) [hieroglyphs] [hieroglyphs] (coffin [hieroglyphs]) [hieroglyphs] (coffin [hieroglyphs]) [hieroglyphs], followed on the cover by [hieroglyphs] [hieroglyphs].

The cartouches of the king have been everywhere destroyed, but the epithet "living for the Truth" is entirely peculiar to Khuniatonu.

5. **Uraeus.**—On the coffin, over the forehead, a uraeus was fixed, emblem of the light that the sovereign, even as the sun, was reputed to shed around him. (Pl. II, Fig. 5.) The snake is in solid bronze ; height 85 millimetres. The greatest thickness of the neck is 4 centimetres. The top of the head is gilded, as well as two vertical cartouches and a series of sixteen narrow scales above which they are placed in the axis of the neck, and also six plaques arranged symmetrically on the sides. The cartouches contain the name of the rayed disc :—

[hieroglyphic cartouches]

6. **Beard.**—The beard, length 0 m ·13, which was affixed to the chin, is of wood, gilt and inlaid with blue and green enamel plaques, arranged in diagonals, chevestred to represent the false plaits that the Egyptian kings, always clean shaven, wore on their chins during certain religious ceremonies.

7. **Flagellum.**—In the closed hands must have been placed the crozier and whip, emblems of the royalty of Osiris, god of the dead, with whom all the dead were assimilated. The crozier and the handle of the whip, which, doubtless, were of gilded wood, have disappeared ; all that remain are the three thongs of the whip. They are three bronze rods, length 0 m ·23 ; on each of them were threaded at least eight small hollow pieces of dark blue glass, in the form of truncated cones, increasing in size from the top to the bottom, and separated from each other by as many pieces of the same shape in gilded wood, almost all of which are destroyed. (Pl. VI, Fig. 3.)

III. ORNAMENTS OF THE MUMMY.

---

8. Crown.—The head of the mummy was covered by way of a crown, with thick gold foil carved in the shape of a vulture. (Pl. XX.) The length from back to front is 24 centimetres, its breadth 21 centimetres. The body of the bird is straight to the front, the head turned to the right ; each foot (the left one is broken) held a ring ♀, emblem of long duration. The wings, instead of being extended horizontally, are raised in a semicircle, so much so that the tips overlap each other, and two rings placed on the outer edge of the wings are superimposed. The whole is of slightly conical form, fitting well to the head ; the empty space between the wings measures 0 m ·115 in width. The lower edges are bent back, and thus form a rim a millimetre in width to consolidate the crown. On the left wing an ancient repair can be seen : the gold foil having been accidentally pierced, the damage was repaired by means of a piece of the same metal soldered below the puncture.

The whole surface is delicately engraved : the details of the head and feet, all the feathers of the body, and the wings with their quills are indicated by lines in repoussé. This piece, unique of its kind, is a magnificent specimen of the goldsmith's art of the XVIIIth dynasty.

9. Necklace.—It has been possible to reconstruct the necklace reproduced on Plate XXI from the gold beads and plaques found in the coffin. The breadth is 0 m ·32, the height 0 m ·565. The details are as follows : Two little bars, each surmounted by a lotus flower formed the ends of the necklace ; these bars are in gold, length 0 m ·09, and form a tube, not soldered, almost square in section, and pierced with six holes for the strings on which the beads were threaded. Upon the tube, at the opposite side to the holes, and occupying only half the length, a triangular piece of gold is attached with a ring at the top to which is fastened a lotus flower in cloisonné ; the calyx is gold, the central petal and those at the sides are lapis-lazuli, the intermediate petals are gold. The remainder of the space is filled with two pieces : one of green glass in the angle ; the other, that which formed the rounded end, was probably of red enamel, but all the plaques are missing.

This necklace consists of five rows of ornaments : the first of these is formed of eighteen plaques of cloisonné on gold, the whole of which is in imitation of the plaited garlands of leaves and flowers with which mummies were surrounded. Each plaque has a tongue-shaped ornament, in three colours : the top is gold, from the centre piece all the inlay has fallen out, but it was probably in carnelian, the lower part has lapis-blue glass. To the left of this ornament a piece of turquoise-blue enamel is fitted, which increases in size at the base in such a way as to fill in the space between the leaves. Four small gold beads are attached to the plaque, two above, two below, through which it was threaded ; beads in blue, green, and red glaze, threaded on the upper string between the attachments of these plaques form, with them, a continuous row of beads. (Pl. XXI.)

The remainder of the necklace consists of hollow gold beads, flat behind, and with a small ring at each end. Of these there are forty-three in the form of a flower-bud ⟨⟩, 21 centimetres in length ; sixteen of the same kind only 17 to 19 centimetres ; fifty-one semi-cylindrical, with rounded ends ⟨⟩, 21 centimetres in length ; and, finally, thirty-four of the same dimensions shaped like flower petals ⟨⟩.

10. Necklace Ornaments.—Small gold and inlaid plaque analogous to those in the first row of the preceding necklace, measuring 18 millimetres in length and 15 in height. The scheme of decoration is twice repeated. It comprises a folded leaf pointed at the tip. The basis is a semi-circle in gold, the remainder being worked in lapis-blue glass ; at the side a small gold leaf contains a model of a flower, of which the calyx is in gold, the corolla carnelian and lapis-blue glass. The empty space between them is filled with turquoise-blue glass ; all the inlays are set into gold cloisons and fixed with blue mastic. The back of the plaque is marked ₁₁₁ᐱ₁₁₁₁, probably to indicate that the piece was the seventeenth of the row. Two gold beads attached to the upper part, and two others at the base kept the ornament in place between two threads.

7

11. Necklace Ornament, hollow, in form of the royal cartouche; vertical, with a ring at top and two at the base; height 0 m ·02, width 0 m ·007. On one of the faces the name of the solar divinity is inscribed in hieroglyphs, stamped in hollow relief ⸱

12. Flower, gold and inlaid.—Piece of jewellery, height 0 m ·035, width 0 m ·027, in the form of the flower symbolic of Upper Egypt. (Pl. V, Fig. 7.) The lower part is a plain gold plaque, the gold calyx is in three striated divisions; the corolla, inlaid with lapis-blue glass, is separated into two parts ending in volutes, whose centres are open. Between these two petals there is a third with rounded top, forming the highest part of the flower, represented by a plaque of carnelian. At both ends a small ring is attached.

13. Beads.—Three cylindrical beads, which have been recovered in fragments; may have belonged to the same piece of jewellery, necklace, or bracelet. The first is in red glass, length 0 m ·023, diameter 0 m ·012; it was covered with gold leaf. The hole is almost square.

The second in lapis lazuli, length 0 m ·022, diameter 0 m ·011, has also a square hole.

Of the third, in green felspar, only one end remains, length 0 m ·018, and 0 m ·01 in diameter, with a round hole 4 millimetres.

Other beads of various shapes and materials have been found, but it is impossible to discover whether they belong to necklaces other than the preceding. There are flowers, ⌒, and ⌒, some *dad*, ⟊, in carnelian, lapis, and light-blue glass. Two other kinds of beads in blue glass must have formed a network laid over the body. One of these has the appearance of an elongated olive pierced with four holes, the others are cylindrical, lined in spirals, bevelled at one end to allow of their being strung together in V form.

14. Fasteners for Earstuds.—The earstuds have not been found, the back parts only remain. These are two gold nails, 32 millimetres in length, the head rounded at the top, flat below, 7 millimetres in diameter, and a stem with a blunt end. The ear ornament must have been in gold and circular in form, having at the back a tube to go through the ear. The heads of these nails, pushed into the tubes, would serve as guards and keep them from falling out.

15. **Piece of Gold Foil, engraved.**—A thick piece of gold foil, 0 m ·018 in height, 0 m ·016 in breadth, which was probably attached to some material. On it are stamped in relief the two cartouches enclosing the names of Aten :

placed together vertically. The shape of the plaque follows the outlines of the two cartouches.

IV. CANOPIC VASES.

SERIES of four canopic vases in alabaster. The embalmed intestines that they contained have perished, and all that now remain are the bituminous rags with which they were padded.   (Pls. VII to XIX.)

16. The Vases, of the ordinary form of this class of object, are 0 m ·368 in height, 0 m ·155 diameter at top, 0 m ·24 at the largest part, and 0 m ·16 at the base.   The diameter of the opening is 0 m ·114, and the depth of the cavity inside 0 m ·34.

The exterior was decorated with a scene, apparently a representation of some personage in adoration before a divinity, but it has been obliterated with such care, that, beyond the outlines of the sign ⊙, no group of the inscriptions is now visible; the sky ⎓, at the top of the picture, was so deeply engraved that it was not possible to erase it, and it has been filled in with pieces of alabaster polished down to the level of the adjacent parts of the vase.

The human heads, which form the covers of the vases, are carved out of magnificent transparent whitish alabaster; height 0 m ·08, of which 0 m ·018 millimetres form the rim that fits into the vase. The diameter at the base is 0 m ·16, and the internal cavity 0 m ·12.

The type is that of a woman, and recalls the portraits of Queen Tîyi, wife of Amenôthes III, more especially the fine head in soapstone found by Mr. Flinders Petrie in Sinai.   The finest of the four heads, which is also the best preserved, has the same elongated face, with the lower part somewhat prominent, and pointed and rather hanging chin, as in the representations of Khu-n-aten, though less pronounced ; the nose is straight and rather shorter than in the three other examples; the cheeks are full ; the eyes, which are long, but not widely opened, are inlaid, the circumference is in blue enamel, the cornea in white limestone, with the corners painted red, the iris in black jasper ; the brows, also in blue enamel, are highly arched. The four faces present almost the same characteristics; in the other three the chin is slightly less elongated, and the face rather broader, making altogether a rounder countenance. The head-dress is a wig, the line of the cap showing on the forehead. Short behind, where it leaves the neck uncovered, it gradually lengthens, and ends in two points touching the clavicles, falling straight down the sides of the face, which it encloses, hiding the ears. It is divided into a number of small coils that fall vertically from the top of the head, except in front where the hair is cut short, and forms three rows on the forehead and on the sides of the face, where the locks are arranged obliquely, and end in an arrangement of five rows, diminishing in length one above another.

On the forehead is a uraeus in alabaster, made of a separate piece fitted into the cover. On all the vases this is broken off close to the surface and only the tail remains stretched out over the head as far as the occiput.

The lower part of the cover broadens out and covers the top of the vase; it is decorated as if it were the breast, with a necklace of three rows of cylindrical beads arranged vertically, and a row of piriform beads. The ornament ⨅ behind serves as fastening and counterweight.

The inscription on the vases having been erased, we do not know to whom this series of canopics belonged. At that period both men and women wore this kind of wig, but the features being feminine and the face beardless, while the heads bear the royal uraeus on the forehead, it may be presumed that these vases were made for a queen, and, in all probability, for Queen Tîyi, wife of Amenôthes III, and mother of Khuniatonu.

V. RELIGIOUS OBJECTS AND AMULETS.

17. Socle of a Statue.—Socle in cedar wood ; length 0 m ·21, breadth 0 m ·138, depth 0 m ·065. It is an unornamented block, with a hollow on the top, 0 m ·09 in length and 0 m ·07 in breadth. The shape shows that it fitted a statue in form of a human mummy, Osiris, Ptah, or a funerary figure.

18. Figurine of Thot.—A small plaque ; height 0 m ·056, length 0 m ·038, thickness 0 m ·006, in greenish glazed pottery, cut out in the shape of the god Thot, a crouching figure turning to the right. The object was broken in two, and the end of the ibis beak is missing. A ring for suspension is placed behind the head.

19. Magical Bricks.—A chapter of the Book of the Dead—the 151st according to M. Naville, the 137th according to Mr. Wallis Budge— prescribes that bricks of unbaked clay, mixed with incense shall be placed in the tomb, towards the four cardinal points. On them were to be fixed various objects, and they should bear certain magical texts. The tomb has yielded the series of four bricks, with the name of Khuniatonu, in more or less good condition, but made on two models.

19a. Northern Brick.—Length 0 m ·18, breadth 0 m ·10, depth 0 m ·045. It. is complete with the exception of a fragment from one end. (Pl. XXII.) It is of Nile mud, sun-dried, the surface washed over with fine greyish clay, lighter than that of which the brick is made. On the top five horizontal rows of hieroglyphs—the ritual text—have been traced in black and then engraved :—

Behind this text there can be seen the hollow which held the foot of a wooden statuette, similar to one found in the tomb of Touiya (p. 29, Pl. 22), and in front the hole left by a peg.

19b. Southern Brick.—Length 0 m ·205, breadth 0 m ·095, thickness 0 m ·04. It is almost intact (Pl. XXII), and is made like the preceding brick. It is inscribed with seven lines of hieroglyphs :—

The end of the first line is covered with a mass of bituminous substance, and the whole of the top of the brick has been soaked with some liquid. In the centre of the space between the beginning of the text and the end of the brick, a twig can be seen inserted in the brick, which has been burnt to charcoal. It is, therefore, quite possible that a small piece of wood was soaked with bitumen and then burnt. I am disposed to believe that after the funeral ceremony, this torch was replaced by a dummy lamp. In the tomb was found an object shaped like a truncated cone, height 0 m ·04, measuring 0 m ·065 in diameter at the top, and 0 m ·03 at the bottom, in green glazed pottery. It had a hole in the middle at the top. (Pl. III, Fig. 1.) This may have been a model of a vase used as a lamp, the flame represented by a twig, which is now destroyed, which would be placed on the brick in order to conform with the prescribed ritual.

19c. Western Brick.—Length 0 m ·09, breadth 0 m ·095, thickness 0 m ·03. The two last bricks are less thick than the first, and they are also in bad condition. On the brick of the west there are five lines of hieratic, traced lengthways; the left half of this object, on which a dad should be placed, has perished. The text transcribes thus :—

19d. Eastern Brick.—Only a fragment of this remains 0 m ·11 × 0 m ·09, thickness 0 m ·026, with only a few hieratic signs of the text

FOUNDATION DEPOSITS.

It is only a very small part of the votive objects commemorating the construction of the tomb that was deposited in this hiding place. The pieces belonging to this category are :—

20. **Four small Alabaster Bricks,** polished on all the faces except underneath ; uninscribed. Their length varies from 0 m ·106 to 0 m ·108, the breadth from 0 m ·031 to 0 m ·032, and the depth from 0 m ·014 to 0 m ·016. (Pl. II, Fig. 7.)

21. **Two Pieces of Red Jasper.**—The first of these, 0 m ·055 long and 0 m ·025 wide, is of oval section and appears to be a pebble, showing no signs of working. The second, 0 m ·065 long and 0 m ·022 wide, is of lenticular section, and the edges, without being sharp, are everywhere regularly fined off. (Pl. V, Figs. 9 and 10.)

22. **Four Alabaster Discs,** the edges bevelled, or rounded below, the top being flat in all cases. Their diameter varies from 0 m ·023 to 0 m ·03, and their depth from 0 m ·004 to 0 m ·006.

23. **Libation Vases.**—Three small libation vases of somewhat rare type, in green glazed pottery, discoloured, 0 m ·11 to 0 m ·128 in height, and 0 m ·059 to 0 m ·066 in breadth. (Pl. IV, Fig. 5.) Here the ordinary libation vase is combined with the emblem of life ♀. The vase, without its foot, takes the place of the handle of the emblem _ānkh_, which it almost resembles in form, although the neck at the top modifies the outline.

24. **Uza (Sacred Eye).**—The Uza, 𓂀 or eye of the sun, the amulet which above all others kept every misfortune at a distance, is represented by a certain number of examples in greenish glazed pottery, that may be classed in seven groups. They were moulded ; some have merely a ring for suspension ; others are in no way pierced, and cannot have been threaded for wear.

First type.—Fifteen examples, length 0 m ·025. The eye is engraved on both sides of the plaque. The white of the eye and the space between the eye and the supporting coil are cut out in open work. The eyebrow is engraved with angulated lines ⟨.

Second type.—Four examples, length 0 m ·035. The eye is only engraved on one side, as is the case with those described subsequently. Here they turn to the right ☥ ; the lower part is open work. (Pl. III, Fig. 4.)

Third type.—One example only, length 0 m ·035. It is a pendant to the preceding ; the eye turned to the left.

Fourth type.—Six examples, length 0 m ·025. Eyes turned to the right, the lower part carved.

Fifth type.—Six examples, length 0 m ·025. Eyes forming pendants to the preceding turned to the left.

Sixth type.—Three examples, length 0 m ·025. Eyes similar to those of the fourth type, but without the space between the eye and its support.

Seventh type.—Five examples. Eyes making pendants with the preceding, turned to the left, and not in open work.

25. Papyrus Stems.—The amulet *uaz* ⌡, which represents the stem of a papyrus, terminating in its flower, assured to the deceased perpetual verdure. Three models of these have been found.

First type.—Two examples, length 0 m ·14 and 0 m ·15. The stem is slender (the largest diameter is 2 centimetres) and flattened. The glaze is bright green, to conform with the regulations laid down in Chapters 159 and 160 of the Book of the Dead, which directs that this amulet shall be made in green felspar.

Second type.—Two pieces, similar but smaller. Length 0 m ·083 and 0 m ·081 ; the stem is round and thin ; diameter 0 m ·013.

Third type.—The eight last examples are more massive, and the green glaze is discoloured. Their length varies from 0 m ·08 to 0 m ·09 ; the medium size of the stem, whether round or slightly flattened, is 0 m ·023. (Pl. II, Fig. 6.)

26. The Mooring Pole.—Amulet in glazed pottery, height 0 m ·165, maximum breadth 0 m ·019 ; represents a post for mooring a boat. (Pl. V, Fig. 5.) The upper part, for 0 m ·04 of its length, is cylindrical. Then comes an abrupt lateral projection, which continues down the length, diminishing in width, giving the object rather the appearance of the blade of a knife. One of the promises made to the deceased was that he should sail in the barque of the Sun ; this post is one of the objects intended for the outfit of the divine mariners.

27. Models of Papyrus.—Sixteen cylinders in glazed pottery, representing rolls of papyrus supplied to the deceased to enable him to read the prayers and incantations required by him. (Pl. II, Fig. 8 ; Pl. V, Fig. 1.) The cylinder has a longitudinal line marking the end of the roll, and, with the exception of the two first examples, a spiral engraved at the ends indicates the coils of the papyrus. These cylinders have been moulded in pairs ; their length is not proportionate to their size.

Their dimensions are as follows :—

2 rolls of 0 m ·10 in length, 0 m ·014 in diameter.
2   „   0 m ·088   „   0 m ·017   „
2   „   0 m ·081   „   0 m ·022   „
2   „   0 m ·08   „   0 m ·018   „
2   „   0 m ·075   „   0 m ·02   „
2   „   0 m ·073   „   0 m ·02   „
2   „   0 m ·064   „   0 m ·012   „
2   „   0 m ·057   „   0 m ·015   „

28. Serpents' Heads.—Three heads of the uraeus serpent, in blue glazed pottery ; these probably formed the ends of magical sticks, the wooden handles of which have perished.

The first measures 0 m ·03 in length, 0 m ·019 in breadth. The eyes are inlaid with carnelian ; at the top of the head there is a square hole for fixing a headdress (disc ?) that no longer exists.

The second, length 0 m ·027, breadth 0 m ·019, has only one eye in carnelian set in gold. A thin stem of bronze passes through the head.

The third, length 0 m ·03, breadth 0 m ·019, still has both eyes in carnelian, but one of the behind extremities is broken. There is no hole in the head.

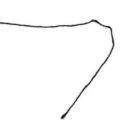

29. Two small Plaques of greyish schist cut in the shape of the amulet Pesesh-kef, which appears to have possessed the virtue of endowing the mummy with power to use the orifices of the body. It is often confused with the headdress *Ten* 𓋽, formed of two ostrich feathers.

The first is 0 m ·13 in height, 0 m ·056 in width at the top, and 0 m ·045 at the base, 0 m ·009 in depth. It is made of two pieces fastened together and arranged thus : .

A column of hieroglyphs on the left side of one of the two faces is this inscription of Queen Tîyi :

The other plaque, 0 m ·138 in height, 0 m ·073 in breadth at the top, 0 m ·058 at the base, and 0 m ·01 in thickness, bears no inscription.

8.

VI. VARIOUS OBJECTS.

30. **Casket.**—Casket in wood with rectangular panels : the cover is in form of a double-pitched roof. The panels are of cedar wood, painted outside in red, framed with strips of black ebony veneer, 0 m ·032 wide. The length is 0 m ·57, the breadth 0 m ·43, the box is 0 m ·27 in height, and with its feet 0 m ·30; the elevation of the cover is 0 m ·09. At each end of the panels there are three slender tenons, fitting into the upright pieces at the corners. These last have perished, but the slips of ebony that covered them remain.

The cover is of the same work; the panels and the triangular pinions are framed with ebony. At the top, near one end of the ridge, a square hole marks the position of a knob.

On one of the sloping sides of the cover, there is a hieratic inscription written in black ink, which transcribes thus : ⸻ "That which is in gold of the household vases." This casket therefore contained pieces of gold plate which have not been discovered.

31. **Fragment of a Piece of Furniture.**—Fragment 0 m ·12 in height, 0 m ·08 in width, part of a piece of furniture. The wood of which it was made was falling into powder and so decomposed that it could only be preserved by covering it with a coating of wax. The cartouche of Queen Tïyi is engraved on it, beside the prenomen of her husband Amenôthes III.

32. Casket in glazed pottery.—Casket in green glazed pottery, discoloured, 0 m ·08, breadth 0 m ·055, height 0 m ·039, and with a cover 0 m ·046, made on the model of wooden boxes. It is supported on four feet; the panels are rectangular, with projecting frames, and surmounted by the Egyptian cornice. (Pl. IV, Fig. 4.)

The cover has a slight pitch, sloping towards the back, with an abrupt drop of a quarter of a circle in front; two small cross pieces are fixed to the under side; one in front, of square section, merely served to hold the cover in place when closed; the other at the back, of this section ⊓, is fitted into a groove in the panel of the box and forms a pivot for the cover.

Two knobs were fixed on the front, one on the lid, the other on the box, and served both as handles and to fasten the casket when it was desired to close it effectually, by tying strings to the knobs and sealing them.

33. Five Caskets in glazed pottery.—The green colour has either faded or turned brown. Simpler in make than the former they have rectangular panels resting on two cross pieces placed at the ends. (Pl. III.) The covers are flat, and have on the lower side two cross pieces, one plain the other bevelled, of varying forms, corresponding with a hollow or projection in the inner side of the back panel of the box.

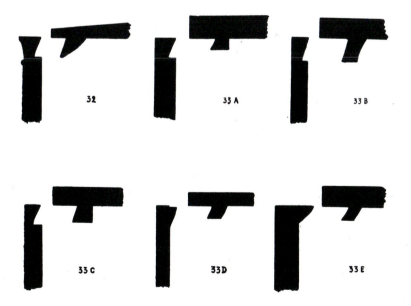

The characteristic features of these five caskets are as follow :—

	Length.	Breadth.	Height.	Height with the Cover.
A.	0 m ·08	0 m ·057	0 m ·047	0 m ·054
B.	0 m ·08	0 m ·051	0 m ·043	0 m ·049
C.	0 m ·078	0 m ·048	0 m ·04	—
D.	0 m ·075	0 m ·044	0 m ·039	—
E.	0 m ·073	0 m ·046	0 m ·035	0 m ·04

All the caskets, except the fourth, have two knobs, one of which is on the cover.

34. Vases in glazed pottery.—The most numerous objects of this find are small cups in the form of truncated cones. They are in green glazed pottery ; in some instances the colour has turned almost white, in others a yellowish brown. It is the shape of vase used for holding fruit, and for drinking cups, as well as for lamps, in which case a wick was burnt in the oil. There are twenty-four cups of this class, more or less high in comparison with their diameter. The largest is 0 m ·073 in diameter at the top, 0 m ·033 at the base, and 0 m ·04 in height ; the smallest 0 m ·045 and 0 m ·024 in diameter and 0 m ·032 in height. The others are of various sizes, the medium dimensions being, height 0 m ·032 and diameter 0 m ·052 and 0 m ·026. (Pl. IV, Fig. 2.)

35. Five small Vases in glazed pottery in the shape of water-jars. (Pl. II, Fig. 6.) The mouth is wide, the contraction for the neck is very slight, the base rounded. Their dimensions are as follows :—

	Height.	Diameter at top.	Maximum Diameter.
A.	0 m ·07	0 m ·029	0 m ·038
B.	0 m ·07	0 m ·027	0 m ·037
C.	0 m ·07	0 m ·027	0 m ·035
D.	0 m ·067	0 m ·03	0 m ·036
E.	0 m ·067	0 m ·25	0 m ·033

It can be seen that the vases have been moulded in two halves, and joined in the baking.

36. Two similar Vases, but the necks are cylindrical and the bases flat.

	Height.	Diameter at top.	Maximum Diameter.
A.	0 m ·08	0 m ·025	0 m ·035
B.	0 m ·08	0 m ·024	0 m ·034

37. Vase, 0 m ·059 in height, 0 m ·028 and 0 m ·038 in diameter at the mouth and the belly, similar to one of the preceding vases without the neck.

38. Two other Vases in greenish glazed pottery, 0 m ·067 in height, 0 m ·024 diameter at the top, and 0 m ·030 diameter at the widest part. The base is pointed and they have no necks, but they diminish steadily in size from the top downwards.

39. Vase Stands.—The preceding vases required stands to keep them upright. Fifteen of these supports have been found in discoloured green glazed pottery : they are rings of rectangular section more or less high in proportion to their size. (Pl. III, Fig. 6.) They can be classified into four different types :—

		Height.	External Diameter.	Internal Diameter.
7	stand	0 m ·008	0 m ·035	0 m ·029
2	,,	0 m ·007	0 m ·033	0 m ·027
3	,,	0 m ·012	0 m ·031	0 m ·024
3	,,	0 m ·012	0 m ·029	0 m ·022

40. Toilet Jar.—One of the most interesting pieces in this find is one in green glazed pottery, now almost white : a statuette of a woman carrying a jar on her shoulder. (Pl. I, Fig. 2.) The total height is 0 m ·077. The socle being 0 m ·026 and the figure alone 0 m ·054 in height, The rectangular socle, 0 m ·036 by 0 m ·023, was made separately, and has two holes in which the feet of the woman were fixed. The vase is spherical and has a wide, straight neck with a slight brim, and a rounded handle on the side. The woman carrying it on her left shoulder is supporting it beneath with both hands, and to restore equilibrium is bending the upper part of her body sharply to the right. This slave is dressed in a long garment without ornamentation ; her hair, which is reddish-black, falls freely round her head on to her shoulders, framing her face. The design is charming, and it is to be regretted that the artist who modelled this piece did not treat it with greater delicacy and more detailed ornamentation.

41. Haematite Vase.—Small toilet jar in black haematite, 0 m ·058 in height, 0 m ·037 diameter at the top, 0 m ·046 in the middle, 0 m ·03 at the base. (Pl. IV, Fig. 3.) The interior is almost similar to the exterior in shape. It is 0 m ·016 in diameter at the opening, and 0 m ·052 in depth ; the lateral groovings show that it was hollowed by a hard stone, worked round the interior by some appliance that wore away the haematite. On the outside three vertical cartouches are engraved side by side. The first ⟮⊙ 𓏏 ⌣⟯, is the prenomen of Amenôthes III. The second contained the nomen of the same king, but during the religious revolution it was so thoroughly erased that now it is only possible to read the beginning of the name of Amon ⟮𓇋𓏏▨⟯. The last cartouche is that of Queen Tîyi ⟮𓇋𓏏𓏏𓄿⟯, wife of this king.

42. Vase in Amazonite.—Vase in the hard stone called amazonite, green with some red and blue spots, height 0 m ·049, diameter at top 0 m. ·047, in the middle 0 m ·043, at the base 0 m ·036. The shape is the traditional one for jars of collyrium. Owing to the hardness of the material the vase has not been hollowed out to the same extent as the preceding one. A mere cylindrical cavity has been bored 0 m ·016 in diameter and 0 m ·042 in depth. (Pl. IV, Fig. 1.)

On the outside is engraved very slightly, the tool having barely scratched the stone, the two cartouches of Amenôthes III.

The upper rim is partly broken away.

43. Glass Vases.—Small vase in white glass, height 0 m ·065, measuring 0 m ·046 in diameter at the opening, 0 m ·052 in the middle, and 0 m ·038 at the foot. It was broken in several pieces, but it has been possible to reconstruct it almost completely. (Pl. III, Fig. 2.) The glass, of a mean thickness of 5 millimetres, must originally have been transparent, but with time it has become somewhat opaque ; in the thinner portions it presents a slightly violet tint denoting the use of manganese to some considerable extent for whitening it during the process of manufacture. The shape is a rounded body, the neck short and widening slightly, a large opening with a plain curved border, the foot shallow. There is no ornamentation.

The fragments of two other vases in white glass were found. One of these is the neck of a bottle 0 m ·04 high; the other, 0 m ·06 high, is part of the body of a vase more elongated than that described above, and must have been similar in shape to the vase in glazed pottery forming part of the signs ♀ on page 28.

STATUETTES OF THE GOD BES.

Among the pieces demanding special notice must be placed two figurines, in glazed pottery, of the god Bes: a form of Horus, who chases evil spirits and guards against sorcery. It is difficult to discover the object for which these figures were made, for the god is not represented under his usual aspect, with hands on his hips as he is when intended for an amulet. As the figure of Bes is often employed as a decoration for furniture and articles of the toilette it may be supposed that these two figures were intended to be used as convenient receptacles for oddments of the toilet table, although the cups they carry would scarcely hold more than a few pins.

44. The first Statuette is 0 m ·102 in height, the socle, rounded at the back, measures 0 m ·035 by 0 m ·038; the god is 0 m ·04 wide across the shoulders and thighs. (Pl. I, Fig. 3.) Bes is represented with his usual grotesque figure: a broad round head with low prominent forehead. flat nose, protruding lips and no chin, great round eyes with eyebrows strongly arched, wrinkled cheeks, lion's ears, hair resembling a mane more than anything else, ending in a point on the back. The belly is distended, the dorsal column is inflected outwards, from it spring five strongly marked ribs, and it is prolonged into an animal's tail which reaches to the ground. This deformed trunk is supported on two bow legs, short and massive, ending in huge feet. The swollen, ill-proportioned arms in front of the chest meet to support a circular dish; this vessel is slightly tilted and the hollow at the top is very shallow.

45. The second Statuette is 0 m ·09 in height and 0 m ·036 broad at the
shoulders. (Pl. I, Fig. 1.) The type is somewhat similar, but of less careful workmanship ; the differences to be observed are that the tongue of
the god is hanging out, his hair terminates in a short plait, turned up
at the end, the ribs are not indicated ; the cup held by the god has
a spout, and in the middle is placed some small round object
indistinctly rendered. An attempt was made to embellish this
statuette, which is in green glaze, with black ; thus the eyes and the
right ear have been painted, but the colour having run and formed
blots behind the head, this ornamentation was not continued.

46. Models of Fruit.—In order to ensure a supply of food for the deceased,
models were placed in the tomb representing bunches of grapes, in
glazed pottery, of which the green colour has now disappeared. They
are ovoid, covered either by squares formed of intersecting lines
engraved on them, or by small circles in imitation of the grapes,
obtained by re-working the squares, or by a mixture of the two
forms. (Pl. II, Figs. 1 and 3.)

Some of these objects have evidently been moulded in two parts.
At the side furthest from the point there is generally a ring for
suspension. Sometimes the ring forms part of a shank which was fixed
into the bunch, sometimes it is a hole bored in a small piece of plastic
material added to the model, and in some cases it is a bead attached
with blue glass. The fifteen bunches found vary in size, the largest
is 0 m ·05 in height and 0 m ·03 in diameter. The dimensions
graduate to the smallest, which is only 0 m ·03 high and 0 m ·018 in
diameter.

47. Models of Knives.—Seven imitation knives, in limestone, of the same
form ⟍ as those used by butchers ; they are implements placed at
the disposal of the deceased for slaying and cutting up any animals
that he might require for food. (Pl. II, Fig. 2.) Their length varies from
0 m ·138 to 0 m ·168 ; their breadth from 0 m ·022 to 0 m ·033.
It is only their outlines that resemble knives made of bronze, and they
are neither sharp nor pointed.

48. Models of Boomerangs.—Fourteen models of boomerangs or curved
sticks for killing birds. The deceased could make use of these in the

Other World to obtain food, or merely for the pleasure of sport. They are in glazed pottery, but the green colour is much faded, and the slight ornamentation drawn in black on the examples reproduced (Pl. V, Figs. 2, 3, 4), is also scarcely visible. There are two types of these weapons. In the first the two extremities are rounded, and the section of the whole length is a very flat oval ; eight of these have been found in lengths ranging from 0 m ·120 to 0 m ·148. The six specimens of the second type are rather more bent, the end nearest the broadened part is rounded, but the haft is of round section and is square at the end. Their length is from 0 m ·120 to 0 m ·158.

49. Handle of a Tool.—Handle of a tool in cedar wood, length 0 m ·16, which must have been left in the tomb by a workman. (Pl. VI.) The section is an oval of 0 m ·026 by 0 m ·023 in diameter, and the edges are slightly concave. One end is rounded, the other is cut straight and has a groove 0 m ·014 in breadth, and 0 m ·024 in depth, for fixing a blade such as a carpenter's chisel.

50. Awl.—Bronze awl ; without a handle ; a squared stem 0 m ·104 in length, pointed at one end. The maximum breadth, 0 m ·004, occurs at about two-thirds of the length. (Pl. V, Fig. 6.)

51. Stone for sharpening.—Block of hard slatey schist, black, which must have been used to sharpen tools. Length 0 m ·178, breadth 0 m ·032, depth 0 m ·02 ; two of the faces are flat, parallel, and terminated in semi-circles.

52. Label.—Small label in cedar wood, of the form ⌂, pierced with a hole at the top, measuring 0 m ·033 by 0 m ·021. On it is this inscription in hieratic, written with black ink 𓏤𓎡𓈖𓏥𓆭 "sawdust of the tree *nozem.*"

53. Head of a Goose in silver.—Fragment of some object, the purpose of which I cannot conjecture. A silver plaque, hollowed into a channel and bent into a quarter of a circle, has fixed to it a small silver tube ; one end of this tube is carried through the open beak of a goose's head, the other end is closed by a strip of bronze ; the top of the head was inlaid. The length is 0 m ·08 the breadth 0 m ·012.

of which may have been flowers and buds. The flowers are composed of a silver calyx with four notches, and a corolla in blue enamel with sixteen sides; the buds have a silver attachment fixed to an oblong carnelian bead.

4. **Gold Ear-ring,** in form of a hollow torus, split at one side, and presenting the cartouche of Tauosrît surmounted by two feathers in gold standing out upon a rectangle of blue enamel.

5. **Pair of small Ear-rings,** of the same kind, without ornamentation.

6. **Parts of a gold Necklace.**—Two flattened tubes pierced laterally with six holes for the threads on which the beads were strung. The four first rows and the sixth were formed of balls in filigree; the fifth was composed of models of fruit (pomegranates) made of beads like the preceding, with the addition of a small tube and ring in imitation of the stem, and a calyx in filigree. The number of beads (84) and of fruits (65) that have been found are not sufficient to reconstruct the necklace in its original condition.

7. **Four Uza,** or Eye of Rā, in electrum, hollow; for suspension to a necklace.

8. **Vase, cordiform,** in electrum, hollow; for suspension.

9. **Two plain Shells,** in electrum, with rings at both ends for attaching them to a necklace.

10. **Five little Figures of the goddess Thoueris,** with hippopotamus body.

11. **Three heads of the goddess Hathor.**

12. **Man kneeling,** holding two palm branches, emblem of millions of years.

13. **Four Flies.**

14. **Three papyrus Flowers.**—All these small objects, Nos. 10 to 14, are in gold, hollow, and furnished with a ring for suspension.

15. **Pair of Bracelets,** silver.—Each bracelet is composed of two plaques joined with a hinge. The front plaque is elliptical, and shows Tauosrît, styled "royal wife," standing, dressed in an ample robe, holding a lotus flower, and pouring the contents of a long slender vase into a cup held by Setuî II. The king is seated on a throne and is holding the emblem of millions of years. At the two ends there are two bouquets of flowers engraved. The hinder plaque has five rows of ornamentation : on the central one flowers are summarily represented; on those at the sides chevrons are arranged in contrary directions.

16. **Pair of gold Bracelets.**—Penannular, of lozenge-shaped section. Round the ends is wound a gold wire, which is twisted into a spiral opposite the opening.

17. **Pair of gold Bracelets.**—A closed hollow ring, of triangular section. On the two lower angles that touch the arm there is an ornamentation of a fillet with small indentations.

18. **Pair of gold Bracelets,** probably for a child. They are plain gold bands, formed into circles with the ends free.

19. **Bracelet in electrum.**—Plain narrow strip, flexible, not engraved, with rounded ends, each pierced with a hole for a string or wire to secure the bracelet round the arm.

20. **Finger Ring,** gold and enamel.—The flat ring has on the exterior a hawk with the solar disc on the head, the wings outspread, and the prenomen of Setuî II in cloisonné enamel. On the inside there is the same bird and the personal name of Setuî II which is merely engraved.

21. **Finger Ring.**—Gold, in open work. The bezel is formed of hieroglyphs cut out and engraved, forming the prenomen of Rameses II, *User-mâ-ré-setep-n-ré mer tanen* : the filigree ring is composed of four groups of the sign of life between two *uas* sceptres placed over baskets.

22. **Gold finger Ring** formed of four parallel wires, with the ends united and milled at the edges, leaving a space between them occupied by eight small ovals arranged two and two in four rows, inlaid with stones or enamel of various colours.

23. Gold finger Ring, double ; made of two rings exactly similar, joined to each other.   The flat bezel presents the cartouche of Tauosrît, surmounted by two feathers and the disc.

24. Double Ring, similar to the preceding, but each cartouche contains only a uraeus with two feathers on the head.

25. Gold Ring.—Plain circle, with a wire twisted round the ends and traversing the movable bezel : a scarab in blue enamel, with a gold band round it, engraved with the name of Tauosrît.

26. Ring, similar to the preceding, but with the scarab in white glazed pottery.

27, 28. Two Rings for a child, of the same form, with broken scarabs.

29. Thirteen thin Plaques in electrum, stamped and engraved with the two cartouches of Setuî II, surmounted by the disc and two feathers.   Both at top and bottom are two stems terminating in rings arranged in such a way that the plaques must have been superposed vertically, and perhaps decorated the links of a girdle.

30–33. Small gold Animals, used as amulets : three lions and a cow with two long feathers on her head, like Hathor.

34. Thin oval Plaque, in electrum, curved, a hole in the centre ; probably covered the top of the handle of a mirror.

35. Two hollow Hands, formed of somewhat thin silver foil, they were possibly mounted on the cover of the coffin.   When found they contained the rings described above.

36. Miniature Sandal, in silver.

37. Carnelian Plaque, carved in form of an ibis, standing ; in front of the bird is an ostrich feather : emblem of truth.

38, 39. Two Plaques in red carnelian, carved and engraved to represent the head of the goddess Hathor. The upper part of one of the heads, which was pierced with a hole for suspension, having been broken, was fitted with a bronze ring.

40. Carnelian, rose pink, carved to show in profile Amon seated; the headdress with two long straight feathers.

41. Serpent's Head in red carnelian, used as an amulet.

42. Long Bead, not pierced, in red carnelian.

43. Jar in glazed pottery, with coloured ornamentation on a white ground. The base is an imitation of an open lotus flower, the petals grey-blue, green, and yellow; near the top the cartouches of Setuî II, surmounted by the solar disc above the sign of gold, are placed between two uraei, of which one has the *pshent,* and the other the crown of the North; the whole is in blue-grey, edged with two rows of yellow that has lost its colour, on which is a fillet of blue-grey.

44. Alabaster Vase, ovoid with straight neck, furnished with two handles in the form of gazelles' heads, and placed on a support also decorated with two handles.

45. Alabaster Vase, ovoid, with a short straight neck, provided with two small handles. On one of the sides is engraved the first prenomen cartouche of Rameses II, above the sign of gold, surmounted by the disc and two ostrich feathers. On the sides are two uraei with the crowns of the South and the North, and also the two eyes of Horus. Below is a garland of flowers beneath which is attached a full-blown lotus flower and two buds.

46. Alabaster Jar with rounded base. Towards the top, filling half the space, three garlands of flowers are engraved, and lower down are the two cartouches of Rameses II surmounted by the solar disc.

PLATE I.

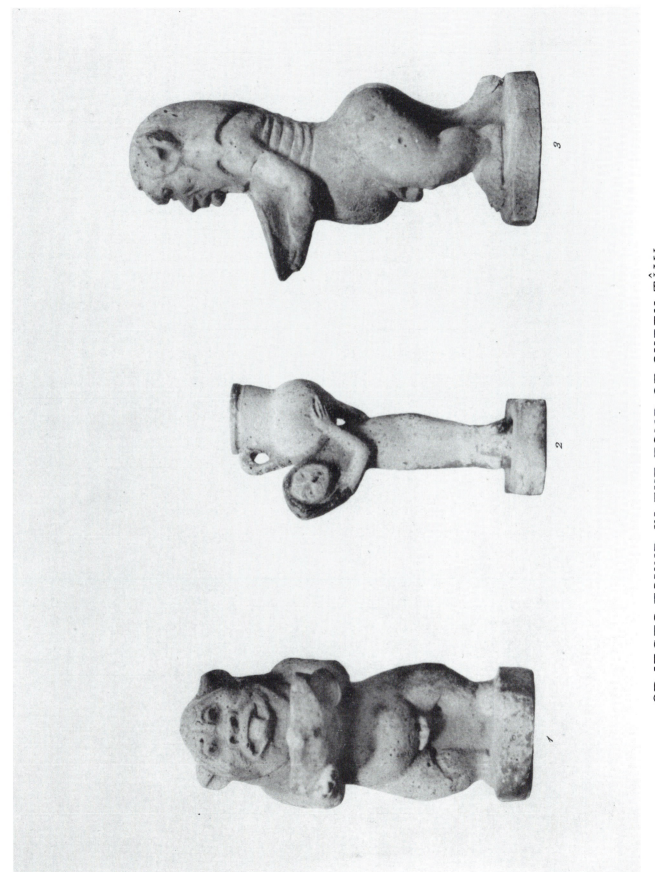

OBJECTS FOUND IN THE TOMB OF QUEEN TÎYI.

PLATE II.

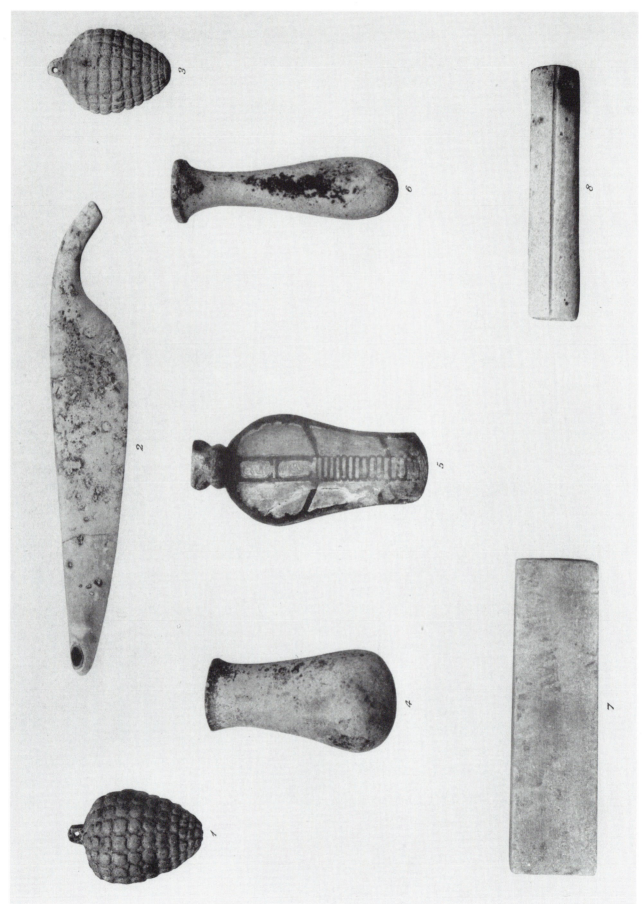

OBJECTS FOUND IN THE TOMB OF QUEEN TÎYI.

PLATE III.

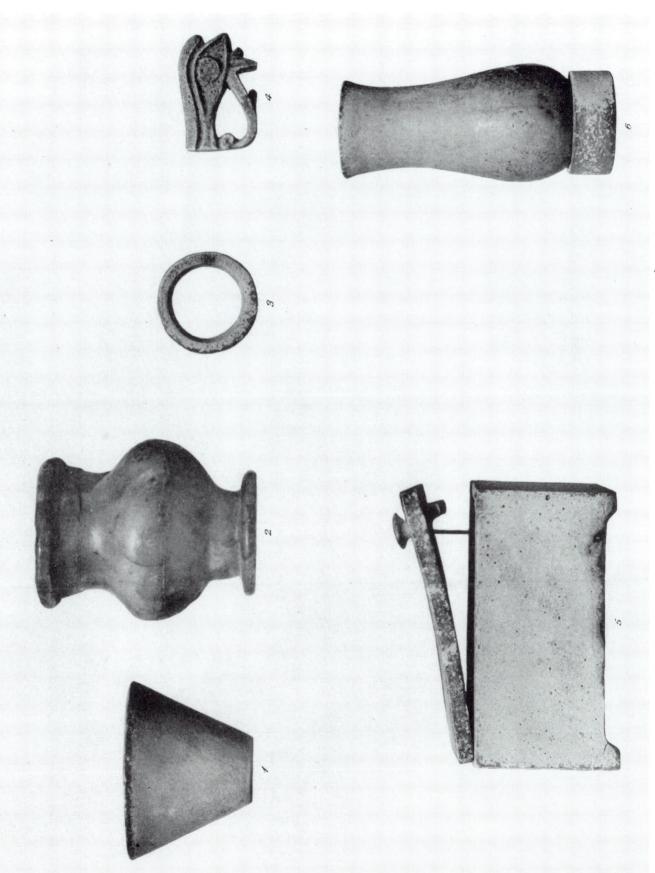

OBJECTS FOUND IN THE TOMB OF QUEEN TÎYI.

PLATE IV.

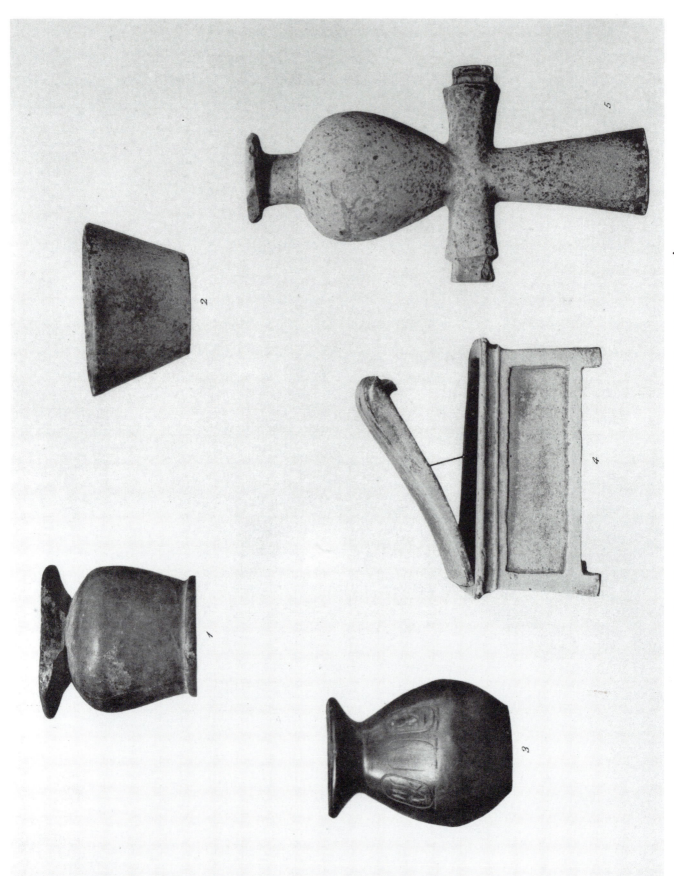

OBJECTS FOUND IN THE TOMB OF QUEEN TÎYI.

PLATE V.

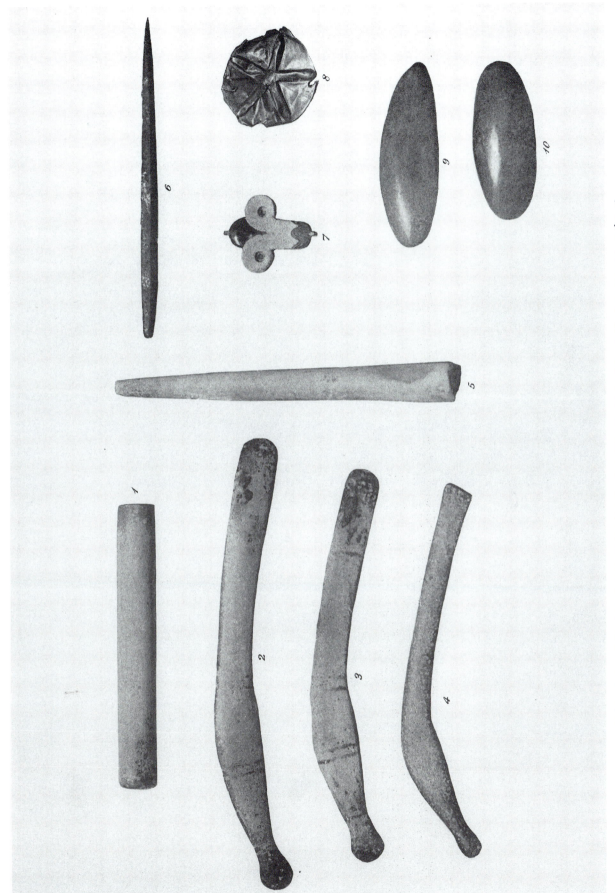

SMALL OBJECTS FOUND IN THE TOMB OF QUEEN TÎYI.

PLATE VI.

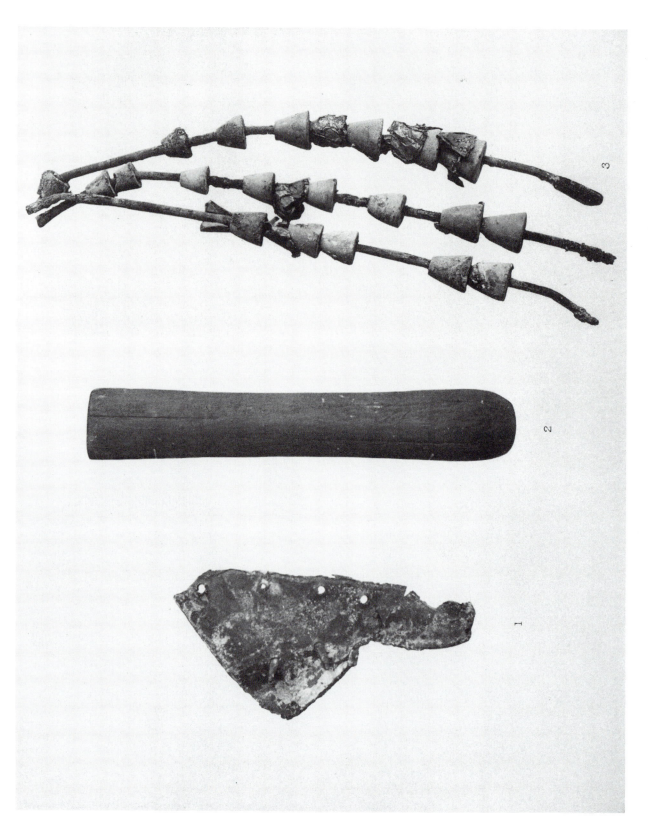

SMALL OBJECTS FOUND IN THE TOMB OF QUEEN TÎYÎ.

PLATE VII.

FOUR ALABASTER HEADS OF QUEEN TÎYI.

PLATE VIII.

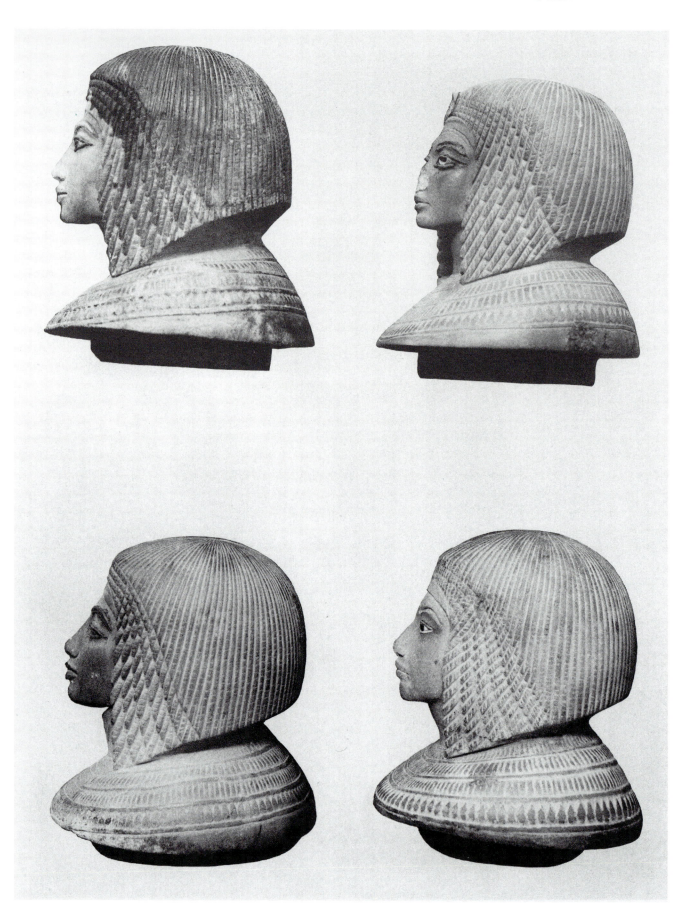

FOUR ALABASTER HEADS OF QUEEN TÎYI.

PLATE IX.

FOUR ALABASTER HEADS OF QUEEN TÎYI.

PLATE X.

ALABASTER PORTRAIT HEAD OF QUEEN TÎYI - NATURAL SIZE.

PLATE XI.

ALABASTER PORTRAIT HEAD OF QUEEN TÎYI·NATURAL SIZE.

PLATE XII.

ALABASTER PORTRAIT HEAD OF QUEEN TÎYI-NATURAL SIZE.

PLATE XIII.

ALABASTER PORTRAIT HEAD OF QUEEN TÎYI-NATURAL SIZE.

PLATE XIV.

ALABASTER PORTRAIT HEAD OF QUEEN TÎYI- NATURAL SIZE.

PLATE XV.

ALABASTER PORTRAIT HEAD OF QUEEN TÎYI-NATURAL SIZE.

PLATE XVI.

ALABASTER PORTRAIT HEAD OF QUEEN TÎYI - NATURAL SIZE.

PLATE XVII.

ALABASTER PORTRAIT HEAD OF QUEEN TÎYI-NATURAL SIZE.

PLATE XVIII.

CANOPIC JARS OF QUEEN TÎYÎ.

PLATE XIX.

CANOPIC JARS OF QUEEN TÎYI.

PLATE XX.

IMPERIAL CROWN OF QUEEN TÎYI.

PLATE XXI.

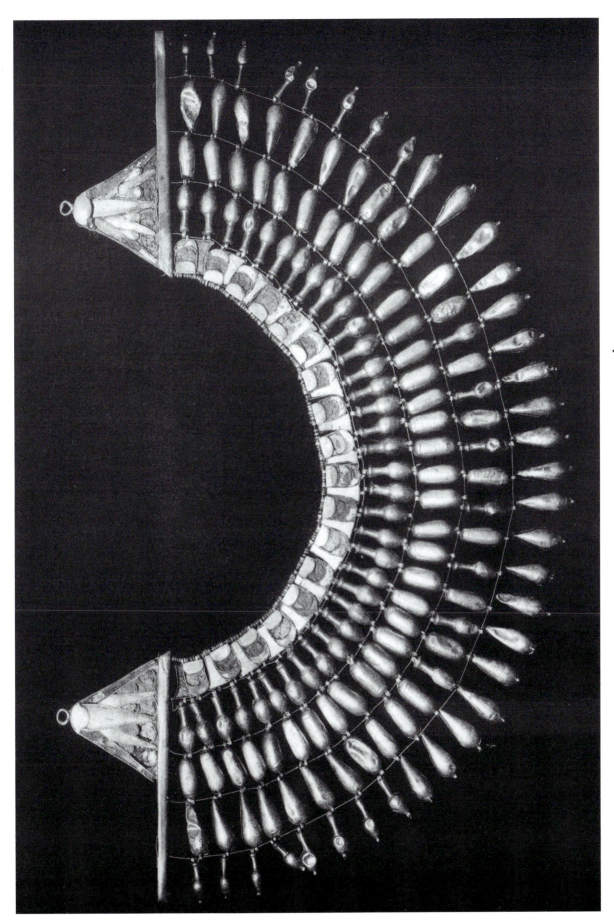

PLATE XXII.

PLATE XXIII.

BRONZE WEDGES.

PLATE XXIV.

PLATE XXV.

SEPULCHRAL CHAMBER, SHOWING ENTRANCE.

PLATE XXVI.

PLATE XXVII.

SEPULCHRAL CHAMBER.

SHOWING SHRINE (DESTROYED) COVERED WITH GOLD FOIL.

PLATE XXVIII.

SEPULCHRAL CHAMBER.

FRAGMENT OF SHRINE.

PLATE XXIX.

PANEL COVERED WITH GOLD FOIL, SHOWING PORTRAIT OF QUEEN TÎYI

AND ERASED FIGURE OF KHUNIATONU.

PLATE XXX.

COFFIN IN SEPULCHRAL CHAMBER.

PLATE XXXI.

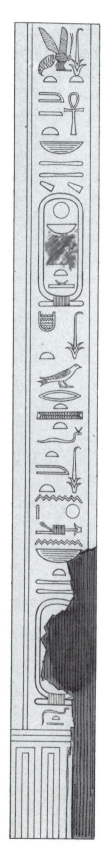

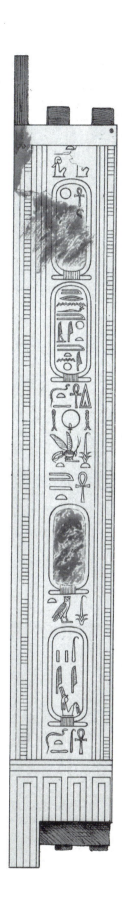

RIGHT-HAND POST AND BEAMS COVERED WITH STUCCO
OVERLAID WITH GOLD, FROM SEPULCHRAL CANOPY

PLATE XXXII.

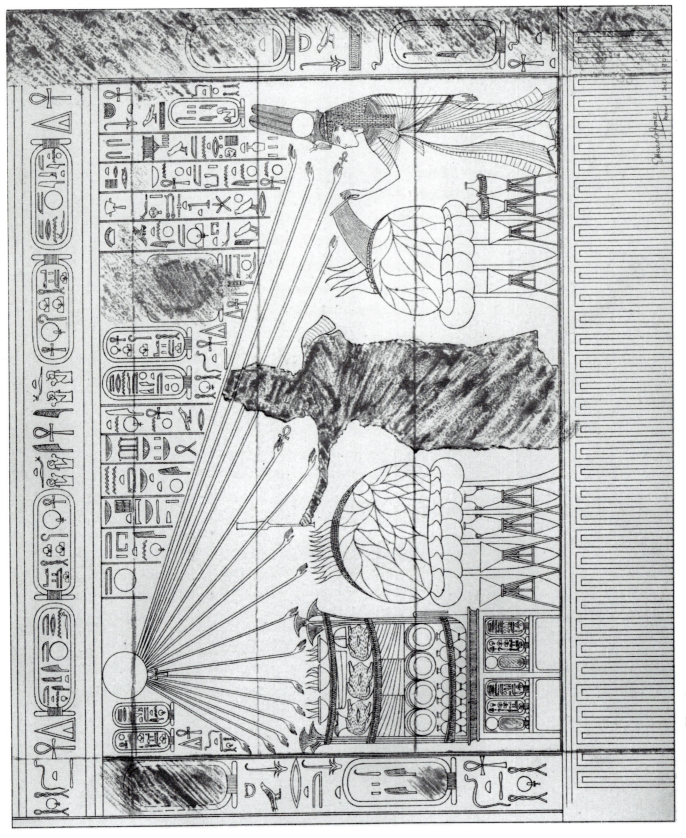

Painted by E. Harold Jones

SIDE OF THE SEPULCHRAL CANOPY SHOWING THE FIGURE

PLATE XXXIII.

Painted by E. Harold Jones

FIGURE OF QUEEN TÎYI

PLATE XXXIV

HEAD OF QUEEN TÎYI,

FROM A STATUETTE, FOUND BY PROFESSOR PETRIE AT SINAI.

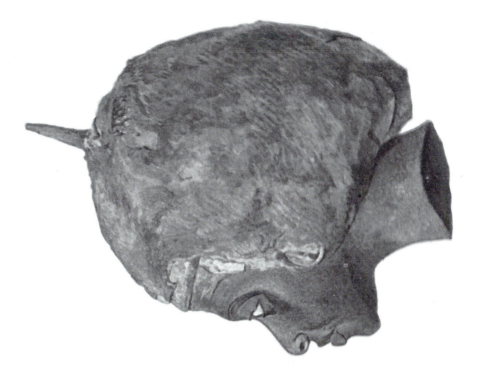

HEAD OF UNKNOWN QUEEN.

(Found in Fayum, purchased by Berlin Egyptian Museum.)
Published for comparison with Queen Tiyi.

PLATE XXXV.